INTO EXTRA TIME

LIVING THROUGH
THE FINAL STAGES
OF CANCER
AND JOTTINGS
ALONG THE WAY

MICHAEL PAUL
GALLAGHER

DARTON · LONGMAN + TODD

First published in 2016 by
Darton, Longman and Todd Ltd
1 Spencer Court
140–142 Wandsworth High Street
London SW18 4JJ

ISBN 978-0-232-53252-4

Thanks are due to David Higham Associates for permission to quote
from *Under Milk Wood* by Dylan Thomas, published by Orion.

A catalogue record for this book is available from the British Library.

Designed and produced by Judy Linard

Printed and bound in Great Britain by Bell & Bain, Glasgow

INTO
EXTRA
TIME

To give light to those in the
shadow of death
And guide them into
the way of peace.
(Luke 1:79)

CONTENTS

PREFACE

The opening words of the original Introduction spoke of my path towards death as highly probable. Now several months later death is certain, a question of months. The story of treatment, remission and then return of more than one zone of cancer is told in the second section of this book. As time has gone on, I often wondered why I was publishing such a personal narrative. It started as a diary for myself, trying to explore my experience of illness. Then I began to think it could be of help to others. But I also fear it could inflate my own fairly ordinary adventure, and I ask forgiveness from those who may find it too self-centred or too pious. It tries to tell the story of a believer going through stages of cancer. If it offers some spiritual light for others in such times of struggle, that justifies it for me.

1
INTRODUCTION

BITS OF AUTOBIOGRAPHY

A year of major change

I am writing this introduction in a strange moment of my life. Indeed by the time this little book finds some readers, I might no longer be alive. I simply don't know. The story is this. In January 2015 I came from Rome to Ireland to give a weekend course but because of heavy bleeding during the flight over, I ended up having emergency surgery the very next day. The surgeon was going on holiday the next morning. So as I came out of the anaesthetic, he apologised for having to tell me that he had found a tumour, and he added that it could be a 'nasty' one. As the weeks passed the nastiness was confirmed, and in May 2015 I completed six cycles of chemotherapy (three days in hospital every three weeks). As everyone knows, this kind of treatment can leave you washed out, suffering from all sorts of side-effects. It happened to me but it was not as bad as I saw in some of my fellow patients. I coined an expression to capture the experience of fatigue and emptiness: *waves of fog.* It is like mist on the hills, which descends unexpectedly, making you lost and disoriented, but then it can lift all of a sudden, leaving you almost normal again. It was an experience of daily insecurity, never knowing when the tiredness would strike and fragility take over. And of course behind the physical experience of unpredictable weakness, like a kind of background music, lay the thought of death looming on the horizon.

Through all these months of vulnerability, often a

13

lonely experience not easily communicable to others, faith was a powerful anchor and source of strength. But don't get me wrong: faith itself often seemed fragile and even unreal. Sometimes people outside faith imagine believers as living within a secure tower of certitude and of consolation. Not so. Even without a crisis of illness, faith is always an adventure of darkness and light, seeing through a glass darkly. And when the shock of a life-threatening disease comes, at least in my experience, both the darkness and the light become more intense.

In this way the outer setting of my life changed radically and rapidly in January 2015. I had been expecting to finish in Rome some six months later but suddenly I found myself back in Dublin full-time and equally suddenly all the commitments for the year were cancelled. The diary was emptied. The shift to inactivity was total. My busy life was over. I adapted to the change fairly quickly. There was little or no mourning over the loss of my previous rhythm of work. A penetrating question came through a friend: could my ease in letting go mean I never really cared? I don't think so. I greatly enjoyed what I was able to do over the years in Rome, in teaching, writing, counselling, guiding a large community, speaking to various groups in different countries. If the letting go was without crisis, I think it came from a sense of realism. I had a serious and life-threatening illness, in fact cancer for the third time in 13 years. The message was clear. The priority was acceptance of this fact and acceptance of being a patient under doctor's orders. No doubt the absence of rebellion or shock came also from a trust in God. Not that I thought the God of life had 'sent' me this illness, but rather that I would be accompanied in this new and perhaps final phase of my life. That was and is the core of my trust and my freedom.

These graces came almost overnight. Without much inner drama, from the day of my operation I accepted that my previous active life was over for good. They say that Pope Francis was a rather withdrawn and unsmiling figure as archbishop in Argentina, but that something of joy was liberated in him on the evening of his election as pope. In a smaller way I know the feel of overnight change. Once I learned that my life was in danger, there came an unexpected sense of peace. Prayer was often easier than before and a quiet awareness of God's presence took over. The well-known psalm 'The Lord is my Shepherd' became my companion even in difficult days of chemo, when of course I experienced something of 'drooping spirit'.

I have no doubt that the previous year was of special importance in preparing me for this situation. Because of age I stopped teaching at the Gregorian University in Rome. I was conscious that I was ending a whole chapter of my teaching life, and threw myself into it with a certain joy. The students (about 200 of them) who knew that it would be my last time, responded with enthusiasm and so I was able to say goodbye to my academic career with much gratitude. I still had another year to do as Rector of a large community of Jesuit students in Rome, the Bellarmino College. There were about 70 youngish priests there from about 30 nationalities. Again I wanted to live this last year with generosity and imagination. The previous years had gone well. I enjoyed offering my services to the community, and in particular I felt it a real privilege to listen to each of them personally at some length. Once again there was an accumulation of thankfulness in me over what life had given me.

Looking back now there was an even stronger gift that came like a crown on the whole year. I volunteered to teach in Vietnam and in the Philippines during July and August

2014. Little could I have imagined how important this short time would be (and how perhaps it could be my last journey of this kind). The weeks in Saigon were intensely blessed for me, with happiness on many levels. Being in a country where Jesuits were so rich in vocations was simply the outer situation. In order to capture something of the impact on me I want to quote some passages I wrote in a journal there or descriptions that I sent to various friends in emails.

> 'The climate here, as foreseen, is hot and humid but air conditioning in my bedroom makes sleep possible for me. In the classroom where I teach for three hours each morning we only have fans, but they provide me with coconut juice. The students unite oriental courtesy and warm Jesuit companionship. I perceive the community here as enjoying a unique mixture of being super organised and super relaxed together. It's the opposite of joyless Western individualism ... I had the adventure of going on the back of a Honda, driven by one of the students, weaving (carefully) in and out of literally thousands of other scooters on fairly narrow streets. Rarely will you find a scooter with only one person on it. I have seen father, mother, and two children more than once. And, like nearly everyone else, I was made to wear not only a helmet but a mouth mask against the pollution ... Even if the outer difficult is challenging in ways, and of course I suffer from a certain linguistic loneliness, the human and spiritual tone of the community is a great source of consolation. If I were ten or twenty years younger, I would probably be asking to stay here or to come back regularly. So this visit is awakening the tired eyes of my heart, like an injection of hope. These days I often

think of the line of the psalm: 'you renew my youth like an eagle's'. I know nothing about the zoology of eagles but I experienced a rejuvenating tonic of renewal here in Vietnam. As good as a sabbatical'.

Yes that Vietnam month was strangely important in preparing me for what was to come.

Some further background

While surviving the impact of six cycles of chemotherapy, I have been reading through old spiritual journals of mine, including handwritten notes covering five decades of religious life. When I was clearing out my room in Rome, and throwing out a lot of stuff, something made me keep these old notebooks, some of them falling apart at the seams. I am glad I did. Not that they are full of wisdom. Many pages are irrelevant now, and some are downright embarrassing in their petty concerns. And yet an interesting story emerges, one of struggles and blessings, and one that changes in tone over the course of time.

I entered the Jesuits at 22 years of age, after doing four years of university studies, three of them in Dublin and one in France. Without that year in France (a period to which I will return) my picture of religious life would have been more puritan and monastic. Even though I would never have put it as bluntly as this, I had tended to look on the 'world' as something to flee from. Only a life separated from the ordinary would be truly Christian. But in France I found a different vision of faith, as a way of living fully within the complexity of the 'world'. The newer emphasis was on the Incarnation as God's embrace of human reality, and for my generation this was confirmed through Teilhard de Chardin's book *The Divine Milieu*. The ripples of this (then controversial) little classic changed the spirituality of the early 1960s, at exactly the same time as the Second Vatican Council. We were able to take a much more positive view of everyday life and action, and of the whole human adventure both personal and universal. Our spiritual transformation would take place not just through prayer but also though the evolving story of each individual. In Teilhard's words 'we complete creation by the humblest work of our hands'. Thus the everyday is the theatre of the Spirit. The French Jesuit also commented on death in words that make so much more sense to me now: 'There is no need to be wildly impatient: death will come soon enough'.

Of course change usually comes about slowly. The ideal goal is one thing and lived realities another. What those journals revealed is that my recurring struggles had to do with personal tensions, insecurities, hurts, loneliness, moments of failure and so on. The blessings were nearly always connected with encounters with people, with times of joy in prayer, with the pleasure of teaching, and with allowing my heart to be changed by other worlds, such as India or Latin America. In fact those changes of tone over the years revealed a lessening of the struggles and an increase of the blessings and their fruits. The frequency of anxiety gave way to a music of wonder and of thankfulness. The struggles did not disappear but a less worried and more serene self came to birth, and perhaps that emergence of freedom prepared me for the challenges I now face.

In other words I face the real prospect of dying within the next year or two, and, as I write these pages, I am revisiting other situations of the past, some of them almost forgotten. Today I read about my sabbatical in Venezuela which included a special month in Paraguay around Easter of 1987. It is extraordinary to recall the details of sleeping in a hut without a door, of hearing oceans of confessions of poor people in the countryside, of finding, in the midst of a corrupt and violent dictatorship, that the gospel came powerfully alive, often through rural bible groups led by women without much education but with great wisdom. Ten years earlier I had spent some months in India (doing what we Jesuits call Tertianship, a period of spiritual renewal usually some years after ordination). India had also been a great experience of challenge and nourishment, working with leper colonies and with Mother Teresa's home for the dying, and even having some time with the great lady herself. But in Latin America I discovered a different dimension of faith and indeed of myself. Here Christianity could hope to have an impact on history. The vast majority of the poor enjoyed strong roots of faith, and many were awakening to the social dimension of the gospel. The welcome I received everywhere, in spite of my imperfect Spanish, transformed my feelings, often leaving me close to tears. The whole period was an experience of liberation of my cramped Western humanity with its focus on the individual (including its centrality in much of the literature I was teaching).

Rereading some of my Latin American memories, I am amazed by the joy they capture. It was such a grace to be thrown into a different world and to have time to meet such a variety of people there. I had forgotten the impact on me of the peasant women who were the real leaders of the faith communities. They carried the burdens of life. They bore the children. They discovered the power of faith and of scripture in a situation of oppression. They became for me a new voice of the social energy of faith. The other group that I remember vividly was the youth, ranging from children to committed young adults and religious. Here I glimpsed real community as the essential seedbed of faith, and also a huge generosity of vision in a world of so much pain. Previously I had done some research on Western unbelief. Now I began to see that faith is blocked much more by lifestyle than by ideas or philosophies.

Rereading those old pages of my diaries put me in touch with the blessings I received, and even though I never returned to Latin America, but moved from Ireland to Italy, I realise that my heart was touched in ways that gave lasting fruit. Even now as the thought of death is my daily companion, I am filled with gratitude for those experiences: 'I thank you for the wonder of my being' (Psalm 138).

Even though I returned to another context in Europe, I realise that these contacts opened new horizons for me. Inevitably I lost contact with some of the social fire but on the level of imagination I was changed for good. It affected even my way of teaching literature when I returned to university in Dublin and later when I taught theology in Rome. I wanted to communicate something of the sheer drama both of literature and of faith, and not simply to offer academic mastery of a merely professional kind. Now that I approach the end of life, I am less shy in saying that many of my students appreciated this and even told me that at times my teaching was challenging to them. For my part I called these moments 'infallibility'! These were times when I knew that I could not go wrong, that I was able to gather a whole vision and to find the right words to capture it for others. I say this not with pride but with reverence, humility, gratitude for the gifts that life gave to me and that people awoke in me. So some of these fragments of light will be gathered later, in the hope of sharing what I have discovered.

BITS OF AUTOBIOGRAPHY

From rereading those pages, in many cases for the first time since I wrote them, a surprising personal insight emerged. As mentioned earlier, I discovered that with the passing of the years I was simply more free to appreciate myself as I am. This was true in various areas of life, from relationships with people to my work as a teacher. In the field of literature, where I did most of my specialised studies, for many years I tried to imitate the style of other professors whom I admired. Gradually I recognised that not only was this making me tense and unnatural, but that the teaching went much better when I trusted my own voice and my own approach. By the end of my career, when I finished teaching theology in Rome at the age of 75, I had become convinced that if I was in harmony with myself, the audience would be at home with me. If I was enjoying myself, the students would also enjoy themselves and gain from it. One of the Ten Commandments says not to 'covet' one's neighbour's goods, and I think this can include talents or even personality. An artist friend of mine says that the most important moment in creating a painting is to look at the frame: within this definite space you have to work. It was a huge relief for me to stop trying to be someone else, and to recognise happily the limits of my own possibilities. Even now it is liberating to admit that my life will have a smaller frame than I imagined a year ago.

The diaries also brought home to me that something of a parallel liberation had happened in my so-called spiritual life. In earlier years I found a recurring complaint about myself: when my prayer lacked intensity, it fell into a kind of routine emptiness. So I moaned about my unsteadiness and spurred myself on to do better. The mistake here was to think that effort was central or that intensity was everything. In my thirty-day retreat in India in 1976,

21

there was a lot of drama and indeed almost daily tears of fullness. This was an important grace at the time (and not so rare in men as might be imagined), but it could not be the measure of prayer in ordinary life. Only gradually did I discover prayer as resting silently but receptively in the presence of God. I had often said to others that prayer means relaxing into the reality of being loved by God, in order to rise into the realism of loving others. But it took many years to embrace this wisdom fully for myself, and now in a situation of illness I am still learning to live its truth. Once again the long-term movement was from anxious self-striving to a trusting acceptance of reality. Indeed I believe that many people, believers or not, travel similar roads towards something of the same serenity and simplicity.

Towards new freedom

In short, the passing of the years, and the action of the Spirit, can lead to new freedom, to trusting one's gift. I discovered an ability to listen to others and to offer a certain healing of their hopes. Gradually dependence on will-power or anxious effort stopped being so central – as if tossed around in the choppy waters of a worried life. When things did not work out perfectly, I became less likely to suffer from self-sulking. Indeed I am convinced that we can all learn to embrace a limited life and find freedom within those limits. If we are at times inclined to see life as a glorious failure, gratitude for the possible can heal all that, creating a music of ordinary wonder. St Paul would go much further: like mirrors we reflect and radiate a light of glory even in this life (2 Corinthians 3: 18). All brings about a new serenity about mortality and a readiness to go home. I wrote after my first operation for cancer in 2002: 'I am amazingly incapable of worry about the future'. That was a moment whose intensity did not last, but it captured a real grace.

I do not want to give the wrong impression, especially to non-believers or those who are less at home with faith. It is not always so easy or clear. Indeed I think my faith has suffered from ups and downs all my life. As already mentioned, since the discovery of my cancer, there are times when it can seem totally unreal. It is as if I stand outside myself and find the whole faith story incredible, distant, infantile. But that is also the source of the difficulty: unless I can be truly 'inside' myself, in touch with depth, so many aspects come to seem distant or lifeless. Friendship, for instance, can lose its salt unless it is nourished through real contact. G.K. Chesterton said with his typical realism that faith involves the art of surviving one's moods. How true! Feelings are important but they are not the key. They come and go. When they are in tune they help faith enormously. But faith has to learn to survive desert moments too.

Here is a good example of the change in overall attitude. I first had cancer 13 years ago, and after an operation in Rome, had six months of chemotherapy. That treatment had much heavier side effects than my more recent therapy, because there have been so many improvements in protecting the patient. But that is not the point here. I recall when I was living with the anxieties of cancer and chemo back in 2002, I sometimes looked at people in the streets around me and said to myself: they are all going to die and they don't know it. I was seeing them from a darker place inside myself. But in recent months, as I have lived with a greater risk of possible death, I found myself looking at people differently. I saw the goodness and the aliveness, as well as the fragile mortality of each one. It was more a matter of enjoying the present moment with wonder, and of hoping that all these people could find their way to true happiness. For some, perhaps through faith in God. But I realise that the school children that I see playing near where I live are not growing up in the world that I knew as a child. Their chance of reaching mature religious faith is shaky. Many will have to make their way in the world without this light. And yet God will be at work in them, guiding them towards forms of love that are reachable for them. If they do not resist, and allow life to prune them of ego, that will be their road of salvation. So something had changed in me over the years. Less worry and more gratitude or gentleness. Less negative judgement and more enlargement of heart. And hence a new freedom, as scripture says, to find peace under 'the shadow of death'. Shakespeare captured the mood perfectly: 'To love that well which thou must leave ere long' (Sonnet 73).

A similar transition happened in my basic images of faith. To put it simply I moved from a rather tight and more anxious model of religion to an ability to find nourishment in a more mysterious and silent love. The philosopher Ricoeur, himself a deeply believing Protestant, criticised false forms of religion as rooted in 'fear of punishment' or else 'desire for protection'. He admitted that atheism could bring about a healthy purging of these immature approaches and open a road towards more genuine faith. I don't think I suffered from that crippling god of fear (although some of the preachers of my childhood were experts in frightening us). But I learned an over-scrupulous concern with rules and conformity. I can see a tendency in me to want personal prayer to be a source of daily consolation. This feel-good temptation has declined with the years and I hope I have moved from religion as a system of order and ultimate meaning (not all wrong but inadequate) to faith focussed on 'Him in whom I have placed my trust' (as St Paul once put it).

There is no denying that faith has made an enormous difference for me in these months dominated by cancer. For instance in late August 2015 when I was enjoying a good period of freedom from treatment and from any symptoms, what the doctors call 'remission', I happened to see a drama on television called *The C Word*. It was an excellent portrayal of the story of a British journalist, Lisa Lynch, who began to write a blog during her battle with breast cancer. It showed all the ups and downs of hope as she went through an operation, chemo and remission. It was honest and moving about the impact on her husband and immediate family. It ended with her being able to have a number of holidays in Spain, but then came the last screen: she died in 2013. I watched this with a personal sense of involvement, and of admiration for her strength. But I was also struck by the total absence of any religious horizon. Before going to bed I prayed, as I always do, the night prayer called Compline. That evening the psalm included the words: 'My God in whom I trust … You will not fear the terror of the night'. And it goes on to promise protection and even 'length of life'. I never ask God to save me from death but that night I prayed the psalm with a huge sense of gratitude for the privilege of faith itself, of being able to say 'you'. Lisa's situation was inspiring but also left me sad. I think that faced with death we are not meant to be deprived of meaning or of Another Presence. I am not of course blaming Lisa. I am simply recording my own amazement about another reality that transforms everything for me. But I stress again that this consolation remains painfully unsteady, alternating between light and dark like a lighthouse. Nevertheless it changes the whole perspective. In fact seeing that TV drama convinced me that my present remission is likely to be temporary. It is a time to be lived fully and fruitfully. So I have written these pages not for myself, not to impress people, but simply with the hope of helping people living through similar situations. This book is also a farewell gift of gratitude for those I have known in all these years, and, I suppose, a goodbye to writing which has been such an important part of my life.

There are various sections in this small book. After this autobiographical introduction, I include two short articles that tell about my interest in unbelief and also a reflection on the prospect of dying. A second section is what I call my 'chemo diary'. I have faced cancer three times in my life and am only too acutely aware that if I had been a poor man in another continent, I would have died many years ago. My hunch is that this third battle will be my last and one that I will lose sooner rather than later. At present, as I write in the summer of 2015, I seem to be in some kind of remission. I was told after a recent scan that the primary tumour in the bladder has disappeared, but that secondaries in the liver are still there, even if reduced in size by the chemo. They will probably return and do so with more force. At present I am living a period of deep gratitude, even of quiet daily wonder that I am here at all and able to enjoy friendships, prayer, energy, writing, music and so much else. At present I am blessed with much serenity about future dangers. Do I have less than a year or more than that? I feel strangely at ease with whatever comes. Of course I am afraid of pain and weakness and impotence. I am afraid of how I will react when things get difficult. I may not be able to write about that experience if it comes. But I was able to keep a personal journal of the time when I was doing chemotherapy and I have now edited it drastically. Everyone knows that it can be a rough experience. So in the hope of helping others facing something of the same challenge, I try to capture those unpredictable ups and downs of body and mood that chemo causes. At the end of this diary, I dare to publish some attempts at poetry, for which I do not claim much talent. Perhaps I started too late in life. Nevertheless these verse texts have been seen by various friends who found that they captured something of the drama of my illness as well as other personal reflections.

Then in a third section I want to offer people some 'fragments and springboards' that I have been jotting down for a year or two now. These are deliberately short explorations of spiritual and religious themes (for the most part). Some may be too simple. Others may be in danger of compressing too much into a short space. Just by being paradoxical, perhaps they can provoke personal reflection in the reader.

As already mentioned, most of these introductory pages are being written while I am enjoying a marvellous period of seeming 'remission'. The chemo is over for now. Energy has come back. I am conscious that this honeymoon cannot last, and so I do not want to waste this precious time. I am living quietly, literally retired not only from my years of work, but from many activities. Occasionally I go out to meet friends or even go to the theatre or cinema. But most days can be almost too calm, with long hours of solitude and no commitments. So I have had to structure the freedom. I read and write for an hour or two in the morning, and again later in the day if I don't have visitors or some outing. It would be more true to say that I reread, because I find great stimulus is revisiting books that I cherished over the years, mainly in literature or in theology or spirituality. This awakens in me a desire to write, to translate in my own way whatever vision I have found. I suppose these pages are something of a personal testament. But that is too solemn a claim. I prefer the expression in the subtitle: jottings along the way.

THINKING ABOUT DEATH

Some of my friends are surprised that I talk about facing death so calmly. Am I telling the full truth? Could I be avoiding the pain by insisting that I am at peace? A good question no doubt, and yet my serenity has remained steady over several months of cancer. At our first meeting I asked the oncologist a straight question, 'If I don't do any therapy, what would happen?' The answer was blunt: 'You would not last six months.' Even then I did not feel panic. A certain hollowness in the stomach, yes. A new loneliness, yes. I wanted to protect others from this news for the moment. But the horizon of faith held strong. Even in the dark I would be accompanied by Jesus. More humanly, I was 75 and had enjoyed a full and varied life. I was about to retire from Rome anyway, after 25 years there. So my sense of peace was rooted both in thanksgiving for the past and in trust for the present and the future.

Of course there were occasional feelings of lostness and alarm, but a freedom to let go seemed stronger and deeper, and this was nourished by finding myself spiritually unalone in facing this moment of life. One of my Jesuit friends, who often drove me to the hospital where I went for three days of chemo every three weeks, once mentioned that it was sad to see me walking through the doors carrying my case. In fact that moment for me was usually one of great consolation because of a sense of the presence of Christ with me. I went through those doors knowing not only that I was not alone, but that the coming days could be strange times of grace – in a spirit of surrender.

Here is another concrete example of what I am

trying to say. After the second cycle of chemo I was well enough to be able to return to Rome to say goodbye to the community (nearly 70 younger Jesuits of whom I had been 'rector' for six years). A practical purpose of the week in Rome was to empty my room. To my own surprise I found myself being happily drastic in my decisions, throwing things out or giving them away. A filing cabinet was full of notes from reading and courses over many years. Almost without thinking about it, I emptied it all into black plastic bags. I had quietly accepted that I would never need this again. In fact it was a joy to see that untidy room gradually become empty, and to return to Ireland with two suitcases (and one small box of books sent separately). The farewell to people was also moving and blessed. I made a fairly emotional speech at a special Mass where I received the sacrament of the sick, asking people to pray for me, not necessarily that I would be healed, but that I could live all this time guided by the Good Spirit.

In this context I have also been thinking a lot about the significance of death, doing some reading about it, and trying to clarify what I believe. It is one of the advantages of cancer that a person has time to reflect, as opposed to a sudden accident or heart attack that can cut life off suddenly.

The prospect of dying

'Let the shortness of life teach us wisdom' says Psalm 89. Dr Johnson famously commented that death concentrates the mind wonderfully, adding, with typical common sense, that a good life prepares us for a happy death. When you find out that death may come soon, it simplifies the focus of the heart. But if, in spite of human weakness, you have tried to live generously, death can often be faced with surprising calm.

Of course there will be some struggle of body and of spirit. There can be shock and anger. Everyone likes to control their life but now I enter a time where control will not work anymore. I face decline, physically but not only physically. As death comes closer, there will be moments of lonely emptiness and of physical dependence on others. The habit of self-sufficiency, so deeply rooted in each person, will fail. Trusting in medical technology will end in disappointment. It can help greatly but this battle too will sooner or later be lost. So I will need something larger and deeper.

Even for someone without a religious faith, it is possible to find quiet strength as death approaches. If you have lived small forms of dying down the years, this letting go will not be totally unfamiliar. Whenever the ego learns self-giving, or experiences love, the muscles of self-surrender have been exercised. In this way you have become used to dying before death itself comes. If your life has discovered love, genuine love that embraces both ecstasy and tragedy, then it has tasted something of lasting joy. Nietzsche once wrote: 'All joy longs for eternity, for deep eternity'. The French writer, Albert Camus, himself an unbeliever, wrote about a capacity to transcend tragedy:

> In the midst of tears, I found within me an invincible smile.
> In the midst of chaos, I found within me an invincible calm.
> In the midst of winter, I found within me an invincible summer.
> No matter how hard the world pushes against me, within me there's something stronger – something better, pushing back.

If we learn to die long before we face death, we are liberated slowly from the pettiness of ego. But faith gives these transformations a whole other context, as part of a divine drama. The biggest difference is that I am no longer alone. Listen to St Paul: 'even though the outer body is wasting away' (2 Corinthians 4:16), 'I know in whom I place my trust' (2 Timothy 1:12); 'He loved me and gave himself for me' (Galatians 2:20). Does this sense of being accompanied by Christ make human anguish easier to bear? Sometimes, but not always. Faith does not suppress physical pain or a sense of helplessness. At times the so-called consolations of religion will seem illusory. But for the believer these times of despondency need not be the dominant music. Beyond fragility lies gift. Faith becomes real as a promise from God: even when you pass through fire, fear not for I am with you (Isaiah 43:2, 5).

The key Christian reality has not been mentioned yet: obviously the Resurrection of Jesus becomes the hinge of history and the source of all our hope. When the Crucified Jesus showed himself to his friends, it was too much to take in. They were overcome with fear and joy together. The philosopher Wittgenstein put it well: 'it is *love* that believes the Resurrection'. And he underlined 'love'. Belief in the Resurrection involves more than a unique physical event. It needs a wavelength of the heart, not just an objective inquiry of the data. We love best when we know ourselves loved. And the Resurrection of Jesus is God's love-pledge to us. It opens a totally different perspective on life and death. It is the ultimate sign that God is always a God of life and always an enemy of death. It offers an explosive new image of who we are and where we are going. We are not made for the finality of death but for fullness of life, here and hereafter. The poet Hopkins captured the novelty and revolution of the Resurrection in these compressed lines:

> Away grief's gasping, joyless days, dejection.
> Across my foundering deck shone
> A beacon, an eternal beam...
>
> In a flash, at a trumpet crash,
> I am all at once what Christ is, since he was what I
>   am, and
> This Jack, joke, poor potsherd,   patch, matchwood,
> immortal diamond,
>   Is immortal diamond.

These powerful words express both an end to mourning or panic, as on a sinking ship, and the experience of a light that changes who I am. If Christ became one of us, and if we now suddenly share in his Resurrection, then we are no longer fragile, useless selves, where humanity seems almost a joke. We are 'immortal diamond', treasures of beauty for all eternity.

For St John that fullness begins here and now. He stresses again and again that 'whoever believes has eternal life' (John 6:47). To believe in Christ and to try to live like him becomes a 'fountain of water welling up to eternal life' (John 4:14). Whatever I have known of love, and whatever I have tried to give in love, makes death less of a break and almost a gentle crossing. The seeds of eternity are already present, burgeoning, giving fruit, and all this is made concrete when we live with love: 'We know that we have passed out of death into life because we love' (1 John 3:14). What God is doing in me here and now, if I receive the gift, is initiating me into a fullness that continues beyond death. The movement towards heaven is already happening.

All that may seem too spiritual when someone is faced with a daily decline of energy. Yet this music of faith can be heard even in dark times. This faith-vision can easily be eclipsed by the weakness or fatigue of approaching the end. We cannot know what it will be like. When I am close to death there may be distress, but I hope to have the freedom to surrender into the hands of God, so that dying can be a prayerful letting go. There may be unresolved hurts or unfulfilled hopes, or worries about those left behind. But gratitude and peace come from having made a difference to some people during your life. And above all from trusting that the Risen Lord may now carry me across the dark threshold. God specialises in resurrection.

The outer process of dying may be frightening, but do I really want to stay here forever? If I listen to my heart, I know I am made for more life than I can yet imagine. When God's promise overcomes my fears, what St Paul calls the 'last enemy' becomes an unexpected friend.

Some theological writing on death seems distant from the drama of dying. Decades ago they talked of the moment of death as the climax of human freedom, where a basic decision can be made about eternity. I find this unreal. The drama of freedom marks all of life but as death approaches freedom can become more limited. The deaths that I have witnessed have been marked by weakness and gentle farewell. I don't imagine that behind the physical decline a person is able for existential options. For myself, I expect to fade away gradually, even to lose the capacity to relate to people around. There may be pain and struggle, but perhaps with quiet trust, I will have the freedom to surrender into the hands of God. I hope my dying can be prayerful in its sinking, marked by a simple attitude of letting go, and with a background music of gratitude. But those theologians were right in one way: one's way of dying echoes one's way of living. If I have lived in tune with Christ, in spite of forgetfulness and sin, I will be free to die in tune with Him.

There is a different theologian who has helped me, William Vanstone, an Anglican who died about 15 years ago. His book *The Stature of Waiting* made me realise a deeper meaning of the word 'passion'. It does not mean only pain but more a state of passivity or 'waiting'. When the Scriptures speak of Jesus being 'handed over', in Gethsemane and elsewhere, he entered not his outer suffering but vulnerability, non-activity, no longer in control. This is an inner quality of going silently towards death, marked by deep trust and by dark glory. It involves more than being active to the end. It is a different surrender to God, more than a sharing of pain. Instead it brings a state of intense meaning and dignity, strangely received.

Over recent months, several friends, knowing I have a potentially fatal illness, have asked me whether I have any regrets about roads not taken. Not really. Certainly the roads chosen could have been travelled in many ways. I could, for instance, have opted for more specialisation in my university work, both in literature and in theology, but I felt called to be a good teacher, without dedicating myself to highly demanding research. I also wanted to be a priest as well as a professor, and the balance there was not always easy. Yes, there were many situations I would like to have lived more wisely. Inevitably I wonder about possibilities that I did not choose, including marriage. There was one special friend, Monique, with whom I lost contact, and even fifty years later I would love to meet her again and know how her life has gone. I can't say with the famous French song that says *'Je ne regrette rien'*, but I can die with no crippling regrets. Gratitude for how life blessed me and allowed me to serve others, that is the dominant feeling, and the one that I hope will accompany me at the end. I include a poem about Monique at the end of the diary section, even though it has nothing to do with the illness.

CONCERN FOR UNBELIEF – LIVING AND COMMUNICATING FAITH

A passion of my life has been to make faith real for people, especially those who find themselves far from church language or what they once knew as religion. I have been blessed all my adult life to have had close friends who were open and unaggressive about their lack of faith. In them I often saw deep generosity and goodness that did me good and that challenged me to live my convictions more fully. The causes of their non-belief varied greatly. Some had scientific reasons for finding God incredible. Others were alienated from and perhaps angry with the church religion of their childhood. Others again were more political, seeing religion as an escape from social responsibility. But many cannot be labelled so easily. Their situation was more of gradual distance than of conscious negation. But all of them were open, at least at times, to honest conversation and none had closed the door to questions and searching. With them in mind, at least indirectly, I wrote various smallish books on faith, starting with *Help my Unbelief*, and then *Struggles of Faith*, *Questions of Faith*, *Clashing Symbols*, *Faith Maps* and *Free to Believe* (perhaps my favourite).

My concern for unbelievers had a definite moment of birth when I was 21, the year before I entered the Jesuits. I spent an academic year at the University of Caen in the North of France. I was away from the Catholic Ireland of my upbringing, and for the first time in my life I encountered widespread agnosticism among my new French friends, most of whom were baptised Catholics. Rather like Monsieur Jourdain speaking prose without knowing it, I discovered myself doing new evangelisation in my own intuitive way. Various kinds of dialogue with unbelievers – usually friends rather than official groups – have marked my priestly life, and it has been an exciting and personally challenging story. Of course the perpetual tussle between belief and unbelief goes on within me. I live a pendulum between grateful fullness and pained murmuring against the strangeness of God. And I am convinced that this fragility is shared by everyone if only they would admit it. This instability is expressed in so many of the psalms and is found in the narratives even of the saints.

In Caen a simple insight was born, one that was strengthened in later years as a Jesuit, working nearly always in university contexts. I became convinced that most blockages to faith were not on the level of truth but on the level of spiritual freedom. This was later confirmed when I studied Newman and discovered his stress on disposition. He insisted less on arguments than on certain inner qualities or attitudes as essential for a genuine search for religious truth: 'with good dispositions faith *is* easy; and without good dispositions, faith is *not* easy'.

A second insight, born from a year in Latin America, was that in western culture our lifestyles, rather than our ideas, determine our religious openness or lack of it. What we call secularisation produces a sensibility of social distance from faith (and the Canadian philosopher Charles Taylor has written brilliantly on this). A third dimension came from my exposure to modern literature: I realised that human imagination is the space where faith is either starved or nourished. The American poet Emily Dickinson expressed it with typical concision: 'The possible's slow fuse is lit by imagination'. In colder words imagination is our faculty of possibility, and if God is the greatest of possibilities, the light of faith needs to explode (Dickinson's metaphor) not in our minds but in our imaginations.

So three topics – freedom, culture, imagination – came to be natural concerns for me, and in this spirit I explored the so-called frontier areas of fundamental theology, my area of teaching in these last twenty years. Perhaps a fourth horizon can be added. Because of many years in contact with students of literature, I was drawn to an existential spirituality of faith rather than to more academic theologising about it, and this remained my focus even when I taught courses on faith and unbelief in Rome. We live a pendulum, as the philosopher William Desmond would say, between astonishment and perplexity. This lived struggle of faith always seemed to me more in need of attention than the doctrinal content. Spirituality comes before theology: if faith is not an experience of encounter, we have little to reflect on except the words of others. And they will ring hollow unless touched by personal fire.

In all this I cannot leave myself out of the picture. My own faith has gone through times of struggle, even if never for long periods or ever arriving at rejection of God. I can resonate with the remark of an Italian bishop, Bruno Forte, that he wakes up every day as an atheist and only gradually climbs into faith. Or again, I am in tune with the claim of the Czech writer Tomas Halik that we need a lot of patience with God, and indeed that unbelievers often lack patience with the strangeness called mystery. So my concern with unbelief connects with the felt fragility of faith as I have known it. Probably the most common kind of 'unbelief' that I experience does not come from arguments or thinking but simply from a spiritual blankness where God becomes 'unreal' (a favourite word of Newman's). At other times God becomes incredible because of the vastness of time and space. Or again, as a friend once put it, 'faith tells a beautifully attractive love story; it makes perfect sense but is too good to be true'. All this tells something about a tug of war inside me, or at least a life-long dialogue of different voices. It is honest to listen and fruitful not to run away. And these tensions over faith have sometimes been intensified in these recent months of my struggle with cancer.

If these are some of the pillars of my reflection on belief and unbelief, what about my own spiritual experience? The answer to that question could seem like self-praise but I offer it as testimony to some threads of joy that have blessed my life, increasingly so as the years went on (as mentioned earlier). There are strands of consolation which leave me feeling both unworthy and deeply grateful. Perhaps the first can be called a gift of healing, but not in any physical sense. Again and again I have been told that I had a capacity to heal people's hope. This was often true in one to one meetings, in spiritual direction, in meeting students, in encounters with younger Jesuits, and so on. I can recall many occasions in Rome when I would bring someone to the door after a conversation, and on the way back to my room I would sometimes drop into the chapel to say to the Lord: 'We did that well together, thank you'. It was the opposite of self-satisfaction. Rather it was a sense of humble reverence, knowing my humanity as the channel of the Spirit's artistry.

Although I am embarrassed in having to say this, I confess that personal prayer has accompanied me through the years, steadily and usually daily. Often it was careless, poorly prepared, skimped, rushed and so on. But it has also been a source of depth, joy, strength and I dare say love. That has been particularly true in this year of serious illness, probably because I had the time and the quiet to enjoy the presence of God. St Ignatius of Loyola surprises people with his claim that consolation is normal and desolation abnormal. He implies that God delights in people, as the Bible says. All I can say is that my everyday times of silence (never very lengthy, often just 30 minutes) have left me blessed and ready for life. And yet they are hard to describe or communicate for others. I usually started from some 'self-gathering'. The other constant was some starting point in scripture. Often just a phrase or two. Enough to awaken a sense of promise and of presence. Then sometimes it was enough to rest there, to let the heart learn in its own way. But the scope of prayer is not rest but movement, change, transformation, ultimately love learned from the action of the Spirit. Before concluding, and following the guidance of Ignatius again, I usually made it more conversational, as if speaking to Our Lady or Jesus or the Father (or some of the Saints). The focus here is to ask more concretely to live what I have glimpsed in the gift of being with God in prayer.

A Jesuit is meant to do an eight-day retreat each year and these have usually been easy and graced times for me. Because of the space, and often with the help of a daily meeting with a spiritual director, the roots of faith can be visited with more intensity. In my experience these weeks were both times of struggle and of great joy, often marked with intense feeling and even tears of fullness. In ordinary or daily prayer one can at times glimpse the glory of God and be overwhelmed with a love beyond all understanding. But in a week of retreat, grace has more opportunity to reach the heart and to deepen realities of faith. For instance, during my annual retreats I learned to pray with a sense of the Trinity. For many people unfortunately this core revelation about God remains painfully distant. For me it gradually became central, even though it is hard to say what I mean. Perhaps I can put it like this. Jesus often went alone into the hills to pray. I imagine him speaking to the Father and being guided by the Spirit. In my prayer I can place myself there with him in the circle of love that is God as Trinity. The Rublev icon captures the unity so beautifully, and there is a fourth place at that table, inviting each of us into that flow of mutual relationship. All this is hard to express, but I have to mention it because increasingly it has been an anchor for me, and more strongly in these months of serious illness.

Let me repeat that I did not always live my ideal of quiet daily prayerfulness. Nor did I always offer my 'gift of healing' with the generosity or reverence needed. If there is a third characteristic of my personal life, perhaps it has been to stand at the crossroads and enjoy the dialogue. This stems from being a Jesuit and yet even in my twenties finding myself moving in the secular setting of various universities. In that setting there was also a desire to go beyond a merely academic approach to literature and to capture something of the drama of lived meaning. This meant hard work: gathering in order to give. If I developed a certain quality of reflection and communication, it was rooted in hours of gathering in order to give. All my life I prepared seriously for any presentations I had to offer, ranging from university lectures to pastoral or spiritual talks. If there was a certain lonely excitement in the gathering, it was replaced by a more relational energy before an audience, or even the invisible audience of a book. My aim was to communicate with a certain imagination and perhaps with a love of words that some say is typically Irish.

But don't get me wrong. This summary of blessings or gifts is not the whole story. It is simply what stands out when I now look back with gratitude and try to capture some of the roots. But you can't have highlights all the time. Most of life is without intensity, and most days are dull and forgettable. And yet any significant change has to show itself here, because the fruits are tested in the ordinary more than in dramatic moments.

Beyond the personal

Perhaps I should mention a larger context beyond the personal. Coming back to Ireland after 25 years in Rome has been surprisingly easy, and yet strange and in some ways sad. In answer to questions over the years I always said that I was 'at home' in Rome but that it was never 'home'. Therefore returning permanently to Ireland was pleasant. In the hospital I could immediately understand the 'subtitles', so to speak, of conversations, for instance light-hearted banter with the nurses. It would not have been the same in Italy. But Ireland has changed so drastically in these 25 years, and especially so in the religious area. I was struck by the often gratuitous cynicism about religion in the mass media. As a priest I sometimes encountered a distance and distrust that was not there before. Not always, I hasten to add. With some of my fellow patients in the hospital I had excellent and honest conversations about faith, even though most of them had moved away from the religion of their childhood. I can understand the new hostility, some of it provoked by the shock of abuse scandals and also by their mismanagement by Church leaders. But I sensed something else: a new spiritual loneliness without roots. Had something precious been abandoned too fast and without much reflection? Could it be a case of throwing out the baby with the bath water? Could we have left behind an unthinking conformism to authority (the Church) only to fall into another (liberal media)? If we cut ourselves off so fast from the wisdom of the past, are we in danger of drifting in an anchorless and adolescent way? Have we bought so fast into a merely functional modernity and its consumer life-style that leaves us humanly impoverished?

These accusatory questions may suffer from a certain hidden nostalgia. Ways of life in Ireland have changed very fast and surely the old situation of a majority Church is not going to return. Passive Sunday practice was never an ideal embodiment of faith. Its collapse may bring a purification, opening to new forms of faith. There is a danger that by trying to hold onto old priorities of Church life we are preserving what Pope Francis has called 'adulterated forms of Christianity'. It is reminiscent of the episode in the gospel when Jesus curses a fruitless fig-tree. History has moved on and a different language is needed, one that does not focus on institutional belonging but on two God-given quests of the human person – their hunger for love and their desire to give of themselves to others.

The images and ideas coming at us from all sides allow little space for God or religion. When do you see a movie where faith has anything but a marginal role? To declare oneself an ex-Catholic is the new normality. Although many declare themselves to be spiritual but not religious, this may mean little more than a vague recognition of a deeper dimension of oneself. But it cannot be dismissed as a sign of a cultural quest. In this scenario if believers are being inclined to close down the hatches and moan, that response would be unworthy of the gospel. Faced with a seemingly hostile context, it is important to discern the spirit of our reactions. If they come from negativity, they will tempt us into defensive and aggressive stances. To echo St Ignatius of Loyola, that could come from the Bad Spirit. Faith calls us to a more creative response to this new situation, but something beyond naïve optimism. As a believer living in a context of unbelief, I am called to grateful living of faith and to mission. Gratitude because it is a blessing to be able to believe in spite of the outer challenges and the inevitable inner fragility of faith. Living out of faith because the gospel vision becomes real when embodied in action, community and service. Mission because we cannot be content with keeping our treasure for ourselves. Even writing these pages is an effort on my part to share that mission.

What to do? How to begin? Everyone knows the reply of a Kerry local to a Dublin motorist lost in side roads, and asking how to get back to Dublin: *I wouldn't start from here*! Something similar can be said of many approaches to faith that people try out today. For instance I would not start from intellectual questioning or lonely thinking. It is often said that recent centuries have unbalanced our use of our brains. Partly because of the huge success of technology, we rely too much on impersonal reasoning (the left lobe) and neglect the deeper and more intuitive roads to truth (the right lobe) that have always guided humanity. If the two hemispheres become divorced, one side falls into cold controlling and the other into soft emotionalism. To do justice to existential questions the two sides need one another, giving pride of place to the personal wavelength and allowing the more logical approach to check it. The question of religion cannot be explored only from the outside. You cannot see the pictures of stained glass from outside the building. All larger issues, such as love or God or life-commitments, need a disposition of openness, wonder and belonging. Openness to imagining a story of transformation. Wonder that liberates from cold logic. Belonging with others in a community of wisdom. Because of our cultural imbalance the temptation is to dismiss all this as out of date, even to scoff at religion as infantile and dangerous. Remembering what Hamlet said to Horatio, 'There are more things in heaven and earth ... than are dreamt of in your philosophy'.

Let us beware of being browbeaten by those who tell us to manage life on a basis of empirical facts and nothing else. Poets and artists of all ages call us not to be ashamed of imagination. And as Chesterton used say, don't confuse imaginative and imaginary. One is a rich road towards fuller possibilities. The other is a trap of fantasy or falsity. Imagination is a great human gift belonging to the right brain. If it is neglected, we become handicapped in our whole approach to life. Religious faith then is off the radar, because it is less a matter of rationality than of receptivity and relationship. William Lynch put it well: faith means imagining life with Christ as the Lord of new imagination.

Plato's famous parable of the cave could be changed and applied to our contemporary context. He pictured people tied up in a cave where they could only see shadows on a wall, which they believed to be reality. But one of the cave dwellers escapes and discovers that these figures on the wall are only shadows of realities outside. Today the dominant illusion is that empirically verifiable facts are the only form of truth. If a contemporary prisoner in this cultural cave were to explore the other world, he or she would discover another level of truth, expressed in intuition, relationship, narrative, poetry and religion. All these flourish through human imagination (provided we can banish the negative echoes of imagination as merely fictitious). But the prejudice of the culture is to see all this as interesting but infantile. In this way we can block out a hugely important dimension of our humanity.

I gave years of my life to studying literature and to teaching it at university level. Looking back now I fear that I often fell into a trap of academic cleverness that robbed me of experiencing the power of the texts themselves. I was trained in Oxford to approach poetry with an almost scientific exactitude. The left lobe dominated the scene. But great works of literature were written with passion rather than precision. It took me years to emerge from the cold schools of literary criticism where I was trained, and to dare to speak more openly of the human drama embodied there. Many people can suffer from similarly cramped ways of approaching all the great issues, including religious faith. If it is approached only from the outside, as cool spectators, we lack the crucial key. Faith starts from a dramatic narrative of God's action. Like literature, it needs a certain quality of receptivity and involvement to come alive. But it is easy to stay aloof or analytical, and therefore to block the possibility of a transforming encounter.

I would love to know how to mend the damage of the lopsided void that makes lack of faith so possible. It would mean healing that one-sidedness in our ways of thinking, and releasing our imagination from its prison of smallness. It would require another language of church, which perhaps is beginning to be found, especially through Pope Francis. It would call for a very different starting point in the journey towards rediscovery of God. I suspect that people need a slower initiation towards depth. It would be something like the 'mystagogy' of the first millennium, when those preparing for baptism undertook a long process of encountering the mysteries. In spite of what I said earlier, I am convinced that people on the edges of religion need spirituality first rather than doctrine or sacraments. Many people who have abandoned contact with church are not convinced or satisfied atheists. Instead they seem to me to suffer from a suppressed hunger for a spiritual dimension in their lives. Malnutrition of inner life lies behind their alienation from religion as they have known it.

How can we retrieve different starting points towards the rediscovery of faith? Only by reawakening contact with the inner self, only by learning to trust again a neglected wavelength of searching, one that pays attention to desire, imagination and wonder as gateways to possible prayerfulness. Perhaps the 'fragments' section of this book is my attempt to awaken some hope for these shy searchers.

In these pages I may have over-emphasised the felt presence of God. Faith is always a mixture of presence and absence. And since the situation of illness meant that I spent a good deal of time on my own, inevitably there were times of emptiness, with a painful sense of God's distance or unreality. The whole Christian story easily seemed incredible and I sometimes felt my fragile life out of touch with these great hopes. What to do in these periods of minor darkness? Resist the discouragement. Build scaffolding of reverence and desire. Wait trustingly. Echoing St Ignatius again, consolation in the sense of a felt devotion or flow towards love, is normal for a believer. It can be intense but more often it is quiet and peaceful. Desolation, meaning getting stuck in negativity, is not from God. It may be caused by my own carelessness, or it may even be a healthy moment of testing and purification. But consolation will return. Therefore have confidence that dawn will come after the dark, and do everything possible to be ready for that return.

A poem to conclude

George Herbert has been my favourite poet ever since I did some research on his work when I was in my twenties. This Anglican priest died at the age of 39 in 1633, leaving behind poems that he described as embodying the 'many spiritual conflicts that have passed betwixt God and my soul'. He brilliantly captured the flux between light and dark, consolation and darkness, and here is a magnificent extract from a poem called 'The Flower':

> How fresh, O Lord, how sweet and clear
> Are thy returns – even as the flowers in spring ...
>   Grief melts away
>   Like snow in May
> As if there were no such cold thing.
>
> Who would have thought my shrivelled heart
> Could have recovered greenness? It was gone
> Quite underground; as flowers depart
> To see their mother-root, when they have blown ...
>
> And now in age I bud again;
> After so many deaths I live and write.
> I once more smell the dew and rain
> And relish versing: O my only light
>   It cannot be
>   That I am he
> On whom thy tempests fell all night.

Just as flowers disappear underground in the winter, we go through times of loss and emptiness. But then comes the miracle of the spring when we 'bud again'. As long as the heart was shrivelled, freshness of life seemed impossible, and now 'greenness' returns. Unexpectedly he rediscovers aliveness to write poetry and ends with a prayer of wonder: how can I be the same person who suffered so many storms in the night?

My paraphrase is tame and weak. But Herbert's text bridges the two areas we have explored – the ups and downs of a struggle with mortality, and also the honest tussle involved in the experience of a believer who always runs into an unbeliever within.

2
FRAGMENTS AND SPRINGBOARDS

These fragments of reflection invite us to ponder on the ups and downs of faith and of prayer. As life goes on many people experience more fog than clarity in their sense of God. But this fragility may be not only normal but fruitful, and the gateway to a different kind of prayer. These sections were written largely during the time of illness but do not focus on that situation.

FRAGMENTS

OPENINGS

Knocking at my door. It is an extraordinary statement: 'I stand at the door and knock.' This is God, being shy, discreet, patient, as if waiting anxiously to be heard. If revelation, as is said, is interruption, this is the gentlest of interruptions, respectful of our slowness and our deafness. While I wander in forgetfulness of who I am meant to be, God stands there hoping for my attention, asking to come in, eager to work a transformation in me. 'The sun is up early and ready to shine in if you open the curtains' (St John of the Cross).

A mutual explosion. But God is at work in us (as St Ignatius insists). Grace transforms. So it is not all up to us. Just the initial opening of a door, the honest asking. Even here the Spirit is prompting us like an artist. Then a flow of love enters, takes over, explodes, and becomes mutual. The impossible becomes possible. 'Not I that live' takes on reality, fire. An intimacy beyond words calls you to rest there, learning how to live and love.

An open temple. The Pantheon is Rome's most ancient building and is famous for an opening to the sky that serves as a keystone for the whole structure. The philosopher Blondel was fascinated by this: it suggested how our lives stay open to another light. One practical reason for the opening was to let out the smoke of ancient sacrifices. So the hole in our ceiling can have a double sense: to let out the smoke of our struggles and, more importantly, to let in the descending light of God's love.

The power of now. That is the title of a best-seller in oriental-style spirituality. It points to a core truth for anyone who tries to pray. Freedom comes when I stop remembering the past or imagining the future. So much of life is preparation (work, meals, meetings ...). To relax into the present is a relief. It becomes a space of restful recognising. It is where healing happens beyond the usual driven life.

Inner journeys. Fortunes can be made nowadays by 'spiritual gurus'. Some draw on Eastern traditions of practical wisdom. Others are more psychological. But they meet a felt need of many people today. They offer advice on finding quiet and peace in the present, especially when the dominant lifestyle leaves people scattered and dissatisfied. Karl Rahner claimed that believers of the future will be mystics or they will not believe at all. He did not mean high mysticism, but simply that people need some inner experience as a ground for their faith. First resist the rudderless drift. Next develop skills of stillness and thresholds of wonder: there is so much more to life. And then you are, as Newman put it, on the 'look out' for a Word from God.

Pointers to God. It's easy to live without God today. He or she seems silent, absent, far from obvious, especially when we are so absorbed in the routine world of each day, or when 'religion' disappoints so many. In older and slower times they used look with wonder at the sky and felt drawn to a Creator. Later thinkers found design in the universe and believed in a Designer. Today they tell us of galaxies billions of miles away and of the universe starting billions of years ago. It is too much. The mind boggles and goes numb. Start from within, many say. Consult your deeper self and its desires. Yes, an important road, but don't get stuck with self.

Hide and seek. (adapting Isaiah 58 and Matthew 25). You try to pray and I seem distant or absent. Am I playing hide and seek? In a sense, yes. My hiddenness is part of who I am. Don't look for feel-good security. When I seem to leave you empty, re-focus. My love is ambitious for your transformation, asking for more than piety. Do I want to be loved in return? Yes and no. Love me first through others, through the forgotten ones. Practice concrete caring. Then come back and you will find me. I will not have changed, but you will hear me say, 'Here I am'. It's very simple: how you live shrinks or expands what you can see.

Spiritual conversation. That was a favourite occupation of St Ignatius of Loyola. There are times when dialogue, between friends, becomes a kind of revelation. We can help one another to pinpoint the movement of God in our lives. We can mirror back to the other person something of their unrecognised riches. We can find fruitful images for our experiences and hopes. We discover thresholds that need to be encouraged into action. The Spirit is transparently at work in such moments of encounter.

DARKNESS

Structures of remembering. Newman once said that we are responsible for the inner attitudes on which faith depends. Why do I sometimes drift through life like an unbeliever? Because I forget to remember. I forget to nourish my recognition of the larger reality that is God with me. I need spaces of focusing. That was the wisdom of the monastic timetable, with set intervals of prayer. Without pausing to 'realise' faith (literally), that whole vision can fade, allowing laziness to invade the imagination.

Fog of fatigue. Bouts of inner emptiness can make faith unreal. Without energy, without the spark of desire, I can sleepwalk through routine prayers. I trust that this dullness of spirit will not last and that God embraces me through this cloud of unfeeling. I often have to live this time in a spirit of self-giving, instead of sulking like a disappointed child. Get on with the daily calls and light will return.

Morning stupor. Psalm 90 recognises a series of daily spiritual dangers, including a 'noonday devil'. Yes there is a dip in energy when forgetfulness can take over. I would add another: the first minutes after waking. I rarely find God easily at this stage. Even if I start some prayer in my head, I get lost and wander around in blankness. Perhaps we wake up as atheists and only gradually climb into faith. For me that possibility comes after the routine of washing, dressing and so on, when I can sit down and relish the gift of this new day. Morning stupor gives way to morning wonder.

Patience with emptiness. Thomas Halik says that atheists lack patience with God, with the pain of silence. You can try to pray and run into a tired void. You need self-patience with your own impotence. That can become a kind of naked faith, tough and toughening. The secret is to not run away. Sometimes, not always, a quiet miracle can happen. The desert makes you ready for life. The darkness can be nourishing – afterwards. You emerge into love, unconscious of its Artist.

Unreal prayer. Newman has a powerful sermon on 'unreal words', about how we can be unpresent behind the words we speak. Something similar could be said of prayer. It risks being a routine gesture, a surface custom. The Hindus have a prayer to be released from unreality into reality. A slow journey, where prayer is my asking and God's doing, carrying me into a larger story, a larger presence of Reality.

The noonday devil. Different moods can make faith unreachable. Hurt by disappointment, we close in like a snail in a shell. Weighed down by failures, we fall into Bunyan's 'slough of despond'. Confused by clever arguments, the whole story seems impossible. Locked into pride Flannery O'Connor's Misfit says: 'I'm doing all right by myself'. And there is another danger that ancient monks called *acedia*, meaning 'without concern or care'. In the desert heat at midday (as Psalm 91 says), the key temptation is apathy or what the Middle Ages beautifully called *wanhope*. Nothing matters. Throw in the sponge. When resistance seems impossible, stop. Recognise the mood. Repeat some favourite words of scripture slowly. The promise of God will penetrate your paralysis, and reborn faith will be humbler and more heart-felt than before.

A divine shyness. God seems too hidden or too different. We easily talk of mystery but it is painful most of the time. God's presence is beyond our usual radar. And that word 'omnipotent' is dangerous. It can suggest a power that intervenes, arbitrary and even moody. But God stands at the door and knocks, asking permission to enter (Revelation 3:15). Christ in some places could not work miracles because of lack of faith. Etty Hillesum voices a surprising truth: 'God, you cannot help us, but we must help you'. I am frighteningly free to hurt the divine shyness. Without our yes, God's Yes remains impotent.

Who is unreachable? Mobile phones give a metallic message: the client is unreachable, please try again later. God can seem like that. I can try to pray quietly, but all I find is a blank, an emptiness. Try again: perhaps that means try differently, in the sense of more hungry, humble, listening from the heart. Less my doing than my waiting. And then a discovery may come: that I was the unreachable one, in my spiritual routines, in my lack of reverence.

Unsteady sea. Chesterton spoke of faith as the art of surviving our mood swings. Why be surprised by the pendulum of the ups and downs of the heart? So many Psalms capture this changeability of our disposition, where God is shiningly present and then confusingly absent. Self-patience is wisdom. But there is something bigger than self-patience – a trust that dawn will come, that light returns after every dark.

Dark faith. Say what you want about peace or joy in believing: faith can be a dark experience. 'Lord, make yourself a little more real.' Let's admit it: faith is more shadow than light, at least in the typical journey of ordinary life. Yes, there are mountain moments, like the Transfiguration. There are times of silent fullness, of rest, grace, presence ... the list is long. They give strength for the daily dullness, where faith can seem like a mist (Vatican I), where loneliness of spirit takes over and emptiness reigns. This is not turmoil. Simply the vision is dim, tired, distant, and one has to wait for light from the mountain again.

Cage of autonomy. I am on a luxury train, speeding through the countryside, checking my emails as I go. My mood is pragmatic. I am cushioned within an illusion of autonomy: I am in control, everything functions smoothly. There seems no need, and even no space, for wonder, for relationship, for prayer. Until we go into a long tunnel and the WiFi collapses. Emptiness invades. All my life I have worked, produced, achieved. But any brush with impotence can break open the cage – to feeling reverence, vulnerability, and the need for Another.

REVELATION

Sensuum defectui. I often sang those words as a child without understanding them. They come from a hymn during Benediction: 'the defect of the senses'. Yes, faith frustrates all external approaches to truth. If reality means only the visible, God remains unreal. If I can only trust what is tangible, God remains painfully out of reach. We are tempted to echo St Thomas: unless I see, I can't believe. It is honest to admit all this and to say with Vatican I that faith can be dark: indeed it can be very dark.

God is useless. This often seems true. God doesn't fit my norms for usefulness. I don't experience miracles. Prayers seem unanswered. 'What does Mr Godot do?' was a question in Beckett's famous play, and the answer is shocking: 'Nothing'. This feeling is one of the foundations of atheism. It happens when they fall into immature images. Our kind of usefulness, not a divine attribute. So instead of constant disappointment, I am invited beyond my easy expectations.

Sed contra: another usefulness. Thomas Aquinas began his discussion of almost every topic with a list of arguments against his own view. Later he answered them: *sed contra, but against this, on the other hand*. Jesus told the Samaritan woman of an inner fountain welling up towards life. God's artistry is here. This is not 'useful' in the usual way, but it is powerfully fruitful. The Spirit guides us, as the companion of my living. Not just in the silence, or the beyond, or the interiority, but in the flow between heart and life, in the long learning of love. That is supremely useful.

Living from a story. The book and film *The Life of Pi* arrive at a crucial moment: which story will you believe? One of grace and miracle, or one of horror and hate? The choice was treated lightly, but the question is real. Faith is a love story, a narrative that gives shape and meaning to life. And more than meaning. It promises companionship, a story that continues in the smallness of each day. 'Not I that live but Christ that lives in me.' Is faith a choice between fullness and emptiness? Not just my choice, as if alone with bleak existence. It is a choice to listen and to trust the story of Another.

A 'gleam of joy'. That is what Tolkien once said was the purpose of his fantasy-narratives. We are led through all sorts of struggles and dangers until we realise that we are not alone and that a deep healing is possible. Gleams of joy happen in many ways. The horizon clears and opens up. Something bigger is glimpsed. My freedom is invited to enter a larger space and call. Faith can often be like that, blessed with times of grace when the fog lifts and a light shines that does not come from me.

The Divine Wedding. Isaiah has an image of God's joy being like a bridegroom over his bride. It is a divine joy about us! But, strangely, the bride had been like a forsaken waste land. It is so real. There is a tired self that cannot open the door to joy. Then God has not only to knock but to push the door. Desolation is dissolved 'like snow in May' (Herbert) by the surprise of the Gift.

The daily revolution of prayer. Prayer is ordinary and extraordinary. Its routine aspects can make me forget the unreality of it. It is unreal in terms of my usual sense of reality – my world of practical externals and human contacts. And when I enter that cave of silence, I encounter a larger Reality. Divine Reality encounters me. In faith I find myself with Christ before the Father. When grace comes and my heart is ready, I know God beyond all ordinary knowing. Yes, prayer is a bewildering mixture of presence and absence. Common sense is overturned. Planning is dismantled. I am led 'by the hand out of the village'.

Enough for me. 'Take and receive', the famous prayer of St Ignatius, ends with the words: 'your love and grace, that is enough for me' (ésta *me basta*). Are we not told that we are restless in this world, because completeness is impossible here? And yet poets, mystics, lovers talk of arriving at a fullness and not wanting anything else for now. Call them times of 'enoughness'. Fragile they may be but they stoke our hope for a love that is eternal.

Sanctity and silliness. Unsteadiness of attention is painful, even humiliating. One moment I can be in harmony and flow, with a sense of not-I-that-live-but-Christ-in-me. And then some minor event pushes me into silliness, drifting, forgetfulness. Is self-patience what is needed when those air pockets happen? Yes, but more so, a humble cry for help-out-of-the-depth-Lord.

From fear to faith. The Bible, they say, has 365 versions of 'be not afraid', as if we needed these words once a day. But Psalm 111 tells us that fear of the Lord is the beginning of wisdom. So there are healthy and unhealthy forms of fear. The serpent tempted Eve to suspect that God was a rival to her happiness and she feared his power. When religion implies God as a punishing judge, people turn away, but Christ revealed the opposite of all this. He invites us beyond being distant servants to become his friends. His Father is close to us in tender mercy. We need to see through shadows of superstition, letting the surprise of faith banish the wrong kind of fear.

Good 'fear'. Young people praise something as 'awesome', when they are struck by what is wonderful or stunning. The word 'awe' hints more at reverence before something majestic. And this is the fear that leads to wisdom. Have you ever been overwhelmed by the glory of God and wanted to remain in silent adoration? An opposite danger is to shrink 'my' God into 'my' smallness. I can sing 'how great thou art' through my little lens. But God is vast, different, ambitious in love, and real prayer shakes me out of pettiness.

Jesus autobiographical. Many sayings in the Gospel reveal the heart of Jesus, his own 'spirituality'. The Beatitudes fit perfectly. They tell of qualities that he lived: a poverty of spirit that trusts in the Father, a welcoming gentleness, a huge forgiveness, a gift of peace, and courage before darkness and danger. Or again the moment when He asks us to take up our cross each day. Prayer becomes an unlearning of falsity and a discovery of a different way, 'keeping our eyes on Jesus' (Hebrews).

Slow learners. The 'learn from me' of Jesus involves a long schoolroom of the heart. This exit from ego is painfully slow. The years are full of discoveries and forgettings, and then remembering again. Biblical expressions of promise find fire and fruitfulness: 'I will not leave you orphans'. 'Remain in me'. Peace for those 'who turn to God in their hearts' (Ps 84). These words become anchors of slow realising. When they echo in the heart I learn to walk through the ordinary – unalone.

SPRINGBOARDS

IMAGINATION

'Spirituality today seems like the Middle Ages without cathedrals: it shrinks our desire for elsewhere' (Jean D'Ormesson). Our 'spiritual' desires can be too small to satisfy the heart. Perhaps they are idols, tempting us to limit transcendence to self-transcendence, just to moments of human wonder? Poetry at its greatest it invites us further. Beauty at its fullest promises another kind of joy. Those cathedrals were maps of mystery and of faith. Over and above their richness of detail, they pointed us beyond ourselves and beyond all we can see here.

'Life is a march through the finite of each day' (William Lynch). A fish breathes air through water, not directly: if it jumps onto a rock and cannot return to the water, it will die. Our natural element is life with all its limitations, and that is home for us now. We can breathe eternity through the ordinary, but if we jump out of the water, escaping the daily drama, we risk unreality. Faith becomes real within the finite situations we live, not by leaping impulsively into the infinite. God liberates us not from time but through time.

'Each person is a half-open door leading to a room for everyone' (Tomas Tranströmer, Nobel Prize-winning poet).

Give thanks that it is not closed. Even half-open is enough to let someone surprise you. Or for you to risk surprising someone. And so the space enlarges. Instead of thinking that migrants should go back home, or the nuisances in my life should disappear, or that I am just a mess, prejudices melt and other eyes take over. It is not only a 'room for everyone' but one where God is smiling because this is a space of salvation. His poem is called 'The Half-Finished Heaven'.

'The text you read is also reading you' (Elmar Salmann). A strange thought, but on reflection, whether it is a biblical text or a poem, encountering a text invites me to enter, to allow myself to be kidnapped. Otherwise I am just skimming it with the surface of my eyes. Quality of attention needs time, courage, and a kind of vulnerability. As in meeting a person at any depth. Or in reading or in prayer. But if I reach a level of presence, little miracles can happen. I am taken out of my small self into an exploration of wonder. I am transformed. The petition of King Lear – 'sweeten my imagination' – is answered.

'The self replaced the soul' (Fanny Howe). This seems a key to 'modernity'. Older periods of human history were more open to mystery, even to the point of superstition. They knew intuitively that life involved more than the visible. They felt themselves in relationship with more than themselves. Then horizons narrowed and the individual self became the measure of reality. In the words of a Flannery O'Connor character, 'I don't want no help. I'm doing all right by myself'. With this self-image God faded or was eclipsed. But it makes a huge difference if another Love is at work. Who would want to exchange 'soul music' for 'self music'?

'What matters is not what happens but how you respond to what happens' (St John of the Cross). Situations can be small or big, but each involves a call. They vary from inconveniences or pleasant surprises to news about birth or even death. My response depends on the wellsprings I live from each day. Self-centred or self 'decentred'? Resisting or welcoming whatever comes? These are dispositions that become habits with the years. Each day is an interplay between God's grace and my response, or better, between God's freedom and my freedom. What emerges, when I allow it, is a shared work of art.

'We have fallen into the mistake of living from our little needs till we have lost our deeper needs in a sort of madness' (D. H. Lawrence). 'What do you desire?' was the first question in the mouth of Jesus (in John's gospel). Each day opens a menu of possibilities. How can I imagine them? As predictable routines plus bits of distraction? Am I imprisoned in smallness of desire? 'To live is to be born slowly', said the French novelist Saint-Exupéry, adding that often Mozart is smothered inside us. Jesus wants to explode my shrunken imagination of how I see everything; what he calls the Kingdom, the Mozart I can daily become.

'And did you get what you wanted from this life, even so? I did.' This is the beginning of a short poem by Raymond Carver. The phrase 'even so' implies that he had a fairly troubled life, including some years of heavy drinking. The next line is *What did you want?* Ponder what my answer might be. Here is Carver's own answer: *To call myself beloved, to feel myself beloved on the earth.* Written when dying of cancer at the age of 50, this simple but deep celebration is inscribed on his tombstone.

'The imagination hadn't awoken. That was his strength' (Graham Greene). This is an intriguing comment on a young murderer called Pinkie in the novel *Brighton Rock*. It was an advantage to avoid conscience, for him to avoid moral issues. Imagination could have disturbed him. Thus imagination is a ladder of possibilities, not just a form of fantasy. It disturbs the imprisoned self. Gift takes over from achievement, when imagination opens to the greatest possibility – being loved by God.

'When people lack a language for depth, life remains trivial' (Dorothee Sölle). Open another door. Escape from the cult of clarity that pretends to be the full story of truth. The opposite of faith is not doubt but a wrong kind of certainty. Blaise Pascal called it the spirit of geometry as against the spirit of finesse. Where can we find a more delicate language in ourselves? When we have an attack of wonder. It can happen through anything that arouses the imagination of newness – drama, poetry, beauty, affection, even trouble or the needs of others. All these open towards another self-listening and towards the possibility of prayer.

'They cannot bear the fullness' (J. H. Newman). He is talking about those who 'merely speak of God' as an idea, acceptable to their own minds. This rational approach is doomed to failure, because it stays safely in the head, tossing words around but far from anything to do with life. Yet everyone has an inner self, inviting them along more spiritual paths, and towards a bombshell that changes the meaning of 'God'. By 'fullness' Newman meant an extravagance of light and love found in Christ. Only a disposition of reverence can prepare us to enter that revolution.

'Only the heart can see rightly; what is essential is invisible to the eye' (Antoine de Saint-Exupéry). This is the 'secret' of the thinking fox in *The Little Prince*. And that story offers other gems. Unless you 'establish ties' with people, you stay invulnerable, but if you come to need someone, he or she becomes 'unique in all the world'. The fox adds that when 'rites' are neglected, no hour is special. A flower explains why humans seem strange to her: because they lack roots, they move around without knowing what they are looking for. Four pillars of wisdom: risk and intimacy; spaces beyond routine; ways of belonging; look beyond the visible.

TRANSFORMATION

'Becoming a person means swinging beyond the habitat of an animal' (Bernard Lonergan). Instead of adapting to the environment, humans are drawn to larger goals. This means a drama of choice, realising that it is (frighteningly) up to myself what I am to make of myself. I become a person mainly through relationships – through being loved, called, sent – by others and by God. Love is a daily surprise, finding oneself recognised as precious. It is also what Jesus did to so many. He recognised their possibilities and gave them a mission. Here the 'swing' beyond instinct reaches its goal.

'If my soul has found you, Lord, why does it not feel you?' (St Anselm). What a real question, part of everyone's experience who tries to pray. We trust that we can find God, or better, that we have been found by God. No doubt we sometimes feel the presence of God. But there is always something more, something unfulfilled. Fullness is fleeting because fullness is, literally, beyond us. God remains beyond our usual ways of knowing, our sensing, imagining, thinking. The great mystics tell about experiences of the night, a painful space where God shines in ways we cannot fathom. You don't have to be a mystic to know what they are talking about.

'To be a saint means to be my true self' (Thomas Merton). Arriving there means a long and bumpy road. A small child seems the centre of its world, and then comes a slow unlearning of that illusion, to emerge into belonging, to others and to God. The onion of the false self has many

layers. If I am not seen as special, I brood and pout. If I don't get my way, I store up my resentment. If someone else shines, I nourish a secret envy. And yet life coaxes the heart to trust in another Love. The years can lead me out of the self-shell and into a liberating surrender. It is a huge relief to stop burning incense before idols of impossibility.

'There can be no knowledge of God before a decision to love God' (Jean Luc Marion). This is hard to understand and harder to live. It can shock us into recognising the difference of faith. Against the temptation to put ourselves at the centre, as judges of reality, instead the question of God needs a Copernican revolution. All the debates about God's existence collapse before the revelation of love. This surprise dismantles our usual inquiries and this gift becomes real only when echoed in our loving.

'One great buzzing confusion' (William James). Is this the whole of daily reality? One thing after another, with little or no connection. Pressure, tension, rush. Even if there are moments of reflection or prayer, what impact can they have on all this confusion? There can be graced times when you rest in silence and sense the love at the heart of everything. But since you have to return to the fragmented world, re-enter it without resentment because it is home. It is where the Mystery glimpsed sends you back to the mystery lived, right there in the flow of complexity.

'Is the eye darkened by its own weakness or else blinded by God's light?' (St Anselm again). Once again we run into the strangeness of faith as an experience. Our serenity

is seldom steady. We live between glimpses of light and surprising dimness, between flow and fatigue. Un-veiled and re-veiled as an Italian theologian likes to say. Because God is always beyond me. And I can also be beneath me, in the sense of not living up to my call. God is not a fact, an object, an ordinary reality. 'God is love' and that revelation should indeed dazzle us.

'*The readiness is all*' (Shakespeare, *Hamlet*). Hamlet has left his dark anxieties behind and discovered a disposition of openness to whatever will come. What he calls readiness is a nugget of spiritual wisdom, with parallels in the gospels. Think of the first beatitude about poverty of spirit, or of the strong words of Mary's *Magnificat*: God will fill the hungry with good things but send the rich away empty. Attitude is all. To be 'rich' is not a question of money but of pride, self-sufficiency, a driven life without needs. What the philosopher Charles Taylor calls the 'buffered self' is someone shielded from wonder or weakness. But to be 'poor in spirit' or 'hungry' means a tone of gentle receptivity. Because the source of strength now lies beyond me. Because to echo Thérèse of Lisieux, all is grace. At the threshold of faith the key is gift, not achievement.

TENSIONS

'Conviction about things unseen' (Hebrews 11:1). This is faith. We stand at a threshold between visible and invisible. Seen realities are powerful around us. Unseen realities can seem simply unreal. A feeling of God's absence is no surprise. It is what we mean by mystery. But beware: mystery is not just negative, a zone of the incomprehensible; mystery is simply too rich for our usual understanding. God remains invisible, painfully so for our ordinary ways of knowing. And yet into that absence comes the presence of Christ, not to abolish mystery but to let us glimpse it in human flesh.

'Christ does not explain our suffering: he shares it and fills it with his presence' (Paul Claudel). When I developed cancer, some people remarked 'You must be asking why me?'. I always replied that 'Why' had never entered my head. A question like that implies a capricious God who zaps people with illnesses. These things just happen randomly. God is the God of life and in Christ death has lost its sting. Even when suffering is terrible, we need not suffer alone. Faith means being accompanied even in the dark, and trusting that 'in all things God works for our good' (Romans 8:28).

'False religion says: "Fear not, trust in God and none of the things you fear will happen to you". Real religion says: "Fear not; the things you are afraid of are likely to happen, but they are nothing to be afraid of"' (John MacMurray). The Scottish philosopher is warning us against superstitious security and pushing us towards

Christian realism. God is always on our side, fulfilling his promises rather than meeting our desires. Death will come someday and many small deaths and disappointments will happen first. According to a biblical image, God is like an eagle, spreading out its wings, protecting its young from falling as they learn to fly (Deuteronomy 32:11). Faith is not a pain killer but a pain carrier.

'God does not protect me but surrenders me to the dangers of a worthy human life' (Paul Ricoeur). We can expect faith to give an impossible security. God promises to be with us, but not to shield us from the ills of life or the dark of death. In shadow times we are accompanied but not miraculously rescued from trouble. Yes, I am protected but not as I might imagine. We are not the makers of our meaning, but we are responsible for the quality of our freedom, for shaping our possibilities, because nobody else can live my life for me. 'For freedom Christ has set us free' (Galatians 5:1). Faith means that his Spirit-artist is at work, even in secret, to guide my choosing.

'A heresy is a half-truth' (Chesterton). Years back Mel Gibson's film *The Passion of the Christ* created quite a stir. It stressed the physical aspect of the passion story, so much so that it fell into heresy. Of course Christ underwent huge pain for us but that was not the key. Gibson forgot that we were saved not by Christ's suffering but by his obedience to the Father and to their merciful love for us. As St Catherine of Siena exclaimed about the crucifixion: 'see how much God loves you'. The film never came even near to that. A heresy is a truth that has lost its friends.

'Have we lost the taste for God, preferring ourselves to God?' (Henri di Lubac). Has our modern way of life locked us into a prison of immediacy? Have we blocked the longing for meaning, feeding us with mere mobility? What could set our imagination free for God? First, we may need to dump out the rubbish, and then revisit our capacity for wonder. A de-tox operation followed by an opening to possibilities. Who can help us in all this? The poets and the poor and our own pain. In different ways they put us in touch with both depth and fragility. 'Stop wandering outside, return into yourself. God was within me but I was looking elsewhere.' St Augustine's dilemma is echoed by today's searchers.

'There is enough light for those to want to see and enough darkness for those with a different disposition' (Blaise Pascal). So many angry tussles take part between heady atheists and rational believers. Pascal would want them to be reverent in their wavelength. As he said brilliantly, when they think they are based on clear arguments, in fact they are guided by fixed attitudes. The gospel itself is full of those who resist Christ, not recognising their prejudices. Jesus did not waste time on the existence of God but on the faith that is born from personally knowing him. Yes, there is enough dark to make you suspicious and dubious, but enough light to let you seek and find if you are open.

'There is no genuine belief without a battle' (Romano Guardini). Faith goes beyond common sense and offers a shock to ordinary thinking. We live with the visible and the practical. Perhaps we don't want to be disturbed by

God. The list of inner resistances to faith is long. And when we come to the content, more trouble arises: stories of miracles; traditions of morality out of touch with today: not to mention Pilate alive and well: 'What is truth?'. And all these battlegrounds may be secondary. The central struggle has to do with Jesus himself, fully human and fully divine. It seems too much to ask, or too good to be true. But if there is a God, and if that God became man, then all the rest is child's play.

'If we deny him, he will deny us. We may be unfaithful, but he is always faithful' (2 Tim 2:13). Warning and hope are contrasted here, surprisingly so. There exists a frightening human possibility of *living* a total NO to life, to love, to God. One can choose this potential hell of a closed self. But there is a huge difference between this option for evil and daily unfaithfulness, like the fragility and forgetfulness found even in saints. Into all this unsteadiness comes a consoling promise: Christ will stay faithful to us, in spite of everything. This ordinary weakness is not a total refusal. This is the adventure of slow learners, accompanied by the patience of God's faithfulness.

'The question "Why must I die?" is a question about life' (Monika Hellwig). This asks what meaning I have found, what values I try to follow, what hopes I have, and whether I am religious or not. But the answer to another question changes the whole horizon: in facing death am I alone, or am I somehow accompanied by God? I am told by St Paul that Christ loved me and died for me, that his resurrection transforms everything, that death has lost its sting, and hence death opens a door into fullness of life.

SPRINGBOARDS

'The most damaging idolatry is not the golden calf but enmity against the other' (René Girard). It is easy to complain about superficial life-styles, or postmodern fragmentation. But a deeper battle remains hidden elsewhere – in our relation to others, or better, in underlying attitudes that become habits of the heart. You probably don't hate anyone, but you can become paralysed by daily negatives. Mini-prejudices and knee-jerk judgements can produce a mood of undeclared war. Across barbed wire fences invisible bullets fly. Loving the other as oneself would be an impossibly uphill climb, unless Christ slowly heals the heart and teaches another possible music.

TRANSCENDENCE

'Whereof one cannot speak, thereof one must be silent' (Wittgenstein). The novel *A Passage to India* satirises 'poor little talkative Christianity'. Do we suffer from too many words and not enough real silence? Is a 'cloud of unknowing' our safest space for God? Yes and no. Yes, because all our language remains inadequate. No, because our searching is not the whole story. The faith story starts from God's searching and speaking. We can never do justice to what we receive as God's gift, but we must try. God's is not what is incomprehensible, but what remains too rich for mere understanding.

'Our greatest trouble and our saving grace is that we have a soul' (Sebastian Barry). What makes us different from animals? The list is long, but to start with: language, laughter, a longing for meaning, and what is called 'soul'. That word suggests self-awareness, and is the source of our wondering, relating to others, and ultimately loving. The novelist Barry is right: we can damage but can also be transformed. We cause suffering to ourselves and others and yet we have the capacity (unheard of in animals) to emerge into forgiveness and healing. That is 'saving grace'. Do we save ourselves on our own? If we recognise this depth called soul, are we not drawn to recognising the possibility of God?

'To complain about the secular world is an own goal' (Elmar Salmann). It seems like the collapse of a whole tradition. Instead of nostalgia for a past chapter of religious history, poverty might do us good. Faith is at home as a

courageous minority, a humble light in darkness. Was it not that way at the beginning, when Peter and Paul ended up in pagan Rome? Today's 'secular' world may not often go to church but there are signs of the Spirit: love of freedom; dignity of the self; pluralism and the other; hopes for justice; value of affectivity; retrieval of the feminine or the imaginative; ecology of the earth. These are treasures of a new sensibility that faith can make shine.

'If I can't be God, I don't want to play' (Janet Soskice). A child sulks when it cannot get its own way. We all sulk in more subtle ways. Pope Francis has criticised the Church for being too self-concerned. 'Modernity' tells us that the individual is everything and that we have to create our own meaning, all of which can leave us self-absorbed – and with more tendency to sulk. What gets forgotten is our human capacity for relating and receiving: Do our hearts not long for openness to others? If we cling to unnecessary loneliness, we continue to sulk long beyond childhood.

'Until your soul is pierced with the difference between your own spiritual capacities and the reality of God, you have not woken up to real religion' (Friedrich von Hügel). Or as Chesterton insisted, Christianity is an outer light liberating us from inner light. Christianity brings (literally) interruption. It breaks into our exploring with a new Word, with the shockingly concrete person of Jesus. And the shock of His 'way'. We could never have imagined that!

'When I regarded Christ as no more than a man of wisdom, I was unable to imagine the mystery concealed there' (St Augustine). It is easy to get stuck at that point. Even believers can reduce Jesus to a model of morality and identify their faith with 'Christian values'. But if we stay with this ethical version of religion, a shadow of sadness falls over the pages of the New Testament. Pope Benedict put it strongly (beginning his first encyclical, *Deus caritas est*): 'Being Christian is not the result of an ethical choice, but the encounter with an event, a person, which gives life a new horizon'. If faith is only morality, we forget the gospel's most personal question: 'Who do *you* say that I am?' Augustine suggested two steps to answer that question and to escape from moral approaches alone: first, go inside yourself, and then ask humbly to know Christ. Starting from reverence you open yourself a 'new horizon' of encounter.

'You were within but I outside'. This is Augustine in Book Ten of the *Confessions.* It captures a daily struggle for roots. So many pulls keep me scattered on the surface and I can begin to resent everything. But this need not be. There is an art of keeping in touch with depth and with God. It involves simply pausing to remember (in Italian *ricordare* means literally 'give back to the heart'). Wisdom needs protecting in the bustle of each day.

'Your life is hidden in Christ' (Corinthians 3: 3). The real faith story remains hidden, invisible, silent, shy. As St Paul says, the mystery was disclosed in Christ. But in each Resurrection appearance Christ disappears into the

unseen and faith becomes fragile again. Nothing about God is graspable in the usual way. Christ remains a Word between two divine silences. What is really happening stays painfully beyond evidence. But there is one concrete verification: we know that we are passing from death to life when we love.

POSTSCRIPT

'I don't know if anyone can be converted without seeing themselves in a blasting annihilating light, a blast that will last a lifetime' (Flannery O'Connor). Like many people I loved this American novelist, who died at the age of 39. She never pulled punches, convinced that you had to shout to reach the deaf. But as I end my own life, I quarrel with her about this famous sentence.

Not everyone meets a Damascus revolution. The Spirit usually works in gradual and gentle ways – in the erosion of the ego in ordinary life, family, work, service, patience in difficulty. And then death arrives as a slow self-losing. You discover that you have been a pupil at a long school of letting go, that has lasted a lifetime, secretly learning from Christ himself. We can join the simpler prayer of Minister Jenkins in Dylan Thomas' *Under Milk Wood*:

We are not wholly bad or good
Who live our lives under Milk Wood,
And Thou, I know, wilt be the first
To see our best side, not our worst.

3
WAVES OF FOG – SHAFTS OF LIGHT

A CANCER DIARY

These pages are selected from a longer diary that I kept over the months of treatment. They start with the day after I arrived from Rome to Ireland in order to lead a weekend course. I had pain and bleeding on the flight and ended up in Accident and Emergency that night. Next day a urologist visited me and, telling me to stop my light breakfast, said he would operate that very afternoon because he was going on holiday the next day. It was all so sudden that I had little time to reflect but I began to jot down some thoughts after the operation.

Discoveries – sudden and gradual

16.1.15

Amazing ... In hospital awake after operation ... less than 24 hours of arriving in Dublin ... full of gratitude and wonder ... and in love with Ireland and its way of treating people, of speaking, of kindness ... Such a relief not to be communicating in Italian even after all these years ... and the operation was so providential ... But deeper a powerful spiritual experience of blessing and the tenderness of God towards me ... and after the operation such thoughtfulness from the surgeon and everyone in the recovery room. I found prayer happening, just as a sense of presence and offering of my years to come. They said that there may be a tumour rather than a stone. But all seems to have been sorted out. Or it may be a battle of life and death again ... [Previously I had cancer twice, in 2002 and 2010.]

18.1.15

I am going through the predictable phases of recovery. After lunch I was exhausted. Lay down and slept deeply and when I came to the tube had no more traces of blood. I had communion this morning and know strongly that 'I am not alone'. There is a new call here to allow God to be tender with me, to understand less, to strive less, to surrender quietly into the silent mystery. I am also deeply aware of the blessings of friends, visiting or on the phone.

19.1.15

... not the easiest day ... It seems a long road to normality. I become impatient and feel fragile. There are some dark thoughts that I may have to cancel my journey to Australia in May. Today is a bit lonely too, listless on various levels.

I am struck by something so obvious. The world goes on without me and will go on without me. So who knows me except God? There is an unreachable aloneness, a core of each person where only God enters to love and create. It is a space of secret, often invisible, belonging or intimacy, where nothing is without meaning, where eternity begins now, where all is being embraced in love. Yes these days are of course intimations of mortality but also glimpses of grace, undramatic but always guiding my life and the world. Even the fact that today I have no visitors and few contacts (some emails) opens this space of realisation.

Sense of insecurity as well as lack of concrete hope. Even this evening's doctor was not very sympathetic or helpful. And then I see a documentary on how 1% of the world own the same as all the other 99%. I am in a privileged place and space.

20.1.15

Still in hospital. Slight fever last night made them keep me another day. I veer between energy and lack of it, physically, psychologically and spiritually. It is a numb time, where I feel the loneliness and yet don't really want to have visitors.

There is a withdrawal process, not having my daily tug of activity, the diary, things to do, and yet not having the strength to do anything very purposeful. I pause and enjoy the Psalms. I am gently touched with a sense of Presence. But it is a strange limbo of waiting and wondering if my normality will ever return in the way I have been used to.

I sense that my previous life is over, or at least that this marks a watershed between my active living, and something diminished in possibilities but graced with acceptance, surrender, even a steadier trust and peace. It seems a turning point in my perspective on my future, which means letting go of the securities of control, planning, preparing. I have not been used to non-energy like this or to these waves of empty time without commitments.

But these days a background music of the Spirit accompanies me when I stop to pay attention. It is more important as serenity and presence than the more difficult moments of longer prayerfulness. At other times God is painfully silent or absent – in the midst of dullness or pain or self-worry. Then God becomes unreal. It is part of the learning, of the mystery, the difference. God is not like that. So I cross the barren deserts and whatever companionship or tenderness is promised is not tangible in any easy way. Perhaps in short moments of light, but most of the time it is fog. As always it is a question of 'patience with God'.

Tonight I feel alone, having been told that I may have to stay until Friday to have a scan. My prayer is simple: *Lord I am in your hands.* I had better be: there are no other hands for me now. But those hands are hidden, and yet the trust is there.

23.1.15

Exactly a week in this room, a week since my operation. I am getting more impatient and frustrated with the waiting for a scan. So after the softer emotions of yesterday, I am more in touch with anger.

24.1.15

Moved to our Jesuit nursing unit. Grateful to be here. On the medical front: Is there more to be discovered in this scan than I imagined? At present I am greatly at peace with any outcome (although I would be horrified by a return to chemo – which I suffered from 13 years ago).

Again the collapse of the routine or structure of my familiar mastery of each day is both a shock and a liberation. I move from ordinary power to relative powerlessness, from confident energy to insecurity and waves of weakness. All this is physical but also psychological and spiritual. And it is a difficult blessing. I cannot plan anything with the same ease or clarity. I have to wait patiently.

31.1.15

Back in hospital since Thursday night. Clot in lung. Yesterday was a day of grace and I wrote to the community in Rome about it. Some remarks from the doctor this morning implied a complicated situation. I went into quiet lonely fear. This could be a long journey, with more passivity. There is an invitation to let go of the control agenda.

Cancer again

2.2.15

The urologist mentioned this morning that the scan showed shadows on the liver and that my whole case would be discussed by a conference of different departments tomorrow. I already had a somewhat sinking stomach this morning but this increased it. The sense of God remains. But there is a new inner weight, a lonely kind of worry. I suppose I am ready to face mortality, but it is almost harder to face a complicated road of treatment. So today was a more difficult day than others. Even physically I felt less energetic, and spiritually less alert. But the quiet trust is there, even if a little dulled.

The doctors just passed by again saying that they will have a meeting about me because 'You have a complex enough history'. OK. But there is another inner history about which the doctors know little.

3.2.15

My old quip about fearing death less than doctors has its truth. The Risen Lord has abolished the old and powerful shadow of death. With Him we are immortal diamonds, as Hopkins says. Fear is inevitable about the smaller things. One fear that comes to me is about faith: I do not feel strong enough to undergo a Thérèse trial of darkness. But there will be flashes of this unreality of God, no doubt.

LATER: Well, the urologist came and was very kind sitting on my bed. But it is cancer. The bladder growth

91

was 'nasty'. There won't be a need to do a biopsy on the liver. An oncologist will come to see me with a plan of chemotherapy. Beyond the facts I am quietly, deeply, surprisingly at ease in the Lord. A good friend was visiting me before and after this news and that helped a lot.

Later on, communicating by phone with various people, I struggled with them to stop excessive worrying on their part.

4.2.15

Whenever my attention turns towards God, I find a sense of presence and peace. This is very nourishing and supportive, and I don't ever remember having such a period of awareness of faith.

First visit from the oncologist, a relaxed man. The cancer is serious. Level 4 (the highest stage). And the liver spots are secondaries. So I am to begin chemo as an in-patient soon, three days of treatment and then three weeks free. I asked if I did no treatment how long would I live: six months. Blunt and sobering. Perhaps I am in mild shock. I went to the hospital chapel and prayed simply: remain in me and we will bear fruit. I know myself accompanied, gently. I feel humanly alone and have decided to tell the full story to very few. In general I'll continue to talk about the bladder tumour. Later on, I can reveal more.

Never has faith seemed so real. This is not out of fear (as some atheists might suspect), but out of a discovery of the quiet reality of God with me in all this.

4.2.15

Back in the community. In Loyola. Extraordinary readings of the day and of martyrs John Brito ... there will be suffering. I hope the heart can stay surrendered when all is difficult. In general I begin to realise that I am entering a whole new scene, a possibly final chapter. I hope the graces of these days can continue: the sense of 'devotion' or familiarity in ordinary prayer. I worry about others, how they will worry and suffer. I want to give of my best to them in these coming months. There will surely be mood swings, from times of tired emptiness and fear to rediscovering the presence of the Lord with me. Even with people, I don't always know how to respond. Part of me does not want long visits, or long conversations. I am easier with long periods on my own, and shorter human contacts. But let us see. Play it by ear.

From time to time I experience waves of unease or lonely awareness: I could be dead within a year, even after cycles of chemo. I have always said that I feared old age and its forms of weakness. But this is sudden and leaves me shaken.

5.2.15

Back in the community. Last night I watched a TV programme made in the North of Ireland called *The Truth about Cancer*. It was beautifully focussed on people, those with cancer and their families. What emerged was a great sense of courage in the face of anxiety and crisis. Much honesty but surprisingly hopeful, even with one lady who was terminal but fighting for patients' rights. I woke up this morning more with a sense of the ordinary journey that I am living. Quietly prayerful, yes, even with moments of emptiness or collapse of energy. But I live with another thought: this day will never come again, indeed by this date next year I might not be alive. More stimulus than sadness or insecurity.

Watched a film *White Elephant* (involving priests in Argentina). At one stage one of the priests says in the film: 'it's your duty to stay alive because people need you'. I am more aware of ordinary life around me and in me. There is drama but in ways death is ordinary.

I find myself going a bit shy with people on the phone or those who want to visit me. My social energy is cautious. I don't want to tell lies but I don't want to tell the full truth widely. Perhaps I am protecting myself from my own feelings too. They will probably emerge in time.

I could imagine writing something on all this experience, if energy allows. But if not, it has been a good life, for which I am immensely grateful, especially for the joy of offering something to people, a kind of wisdom or healing of hope. I wrote to Jesuit friends in Vietnam. One reply was very warm and personal, assuming that I may not win this battle. That's okay with me. It's a very possible truth and I can live with it day by day.

Watching rugby on TV with the full community, I thought of the phrase 'in the midst of life we are in death'. Later I found that it comes from the Anglican burial service but translates an older Latin antiphon '*media vita in morte sumus*'. It seemed to capture my experience of remembering my situation in the middle of doing something ordinary (like TV). It invites me into a different awareness, sometimes with a sinking feeling of helplessness, but more often with a quiet sense of something deeper happening and of God gently accompanying me in this strange and daily movement towards mortality.

7.2.15

Yes, I would like to write a book about all this, to be published even after my death. I hope some reflections that this situation provokes in me could be of help to others. Let us see.

On reflection, is 'in the midst of life we are in death' the full Christian story? Not really. That phrase has no room for the revolution of the Resurrection. In a real sense we are no longer 'in death', dominated by the shadow of our mortality. When the shocked disciples of Jesus encountered the second shock of his being alive, it exploded all previous images of life and of death. Death where is your sting? Every culture in history tried to cope with the dark inevitability of death. I have to do the same. But there is an extraordinary change of scene, of meaning, of possibility. We now know that God has nothing to do with death any more. That with the Resurrection of Jesus a whole other door opens. So we could change that old saying, 'in the midst of death we are called into life'.

I have time, enforced time, for plenty of that kind of reflection. Big time, as they say! What comes to me today is the dialogue between promise and the present moment. I live in the present moment, when the signs of illness are few, where I have the chance to listen to feelings and desires. But there is the larger horizon of promise, God's promise to be with us, with me, as a guide through all deserts and towards a fullness beyond all imagining. That is more than enough as an anchor for now.

I read some internet stuff on reactions to the news of cancer and of possible death. I don't recognise myself in most of it: denial, anger and so on. But I do think that the classic advice is good – to find some people to talk to openly about reactions and emotions. After all, that would be in keeping with the Jesuit tradition of spiritual conversation.

People say I look really well at present. Rested and relaxed. Even for myself there are few tangible signs of illness. Yes, easily tired, slowing down, some minor pain. For other people it is hard to imagine that the enemy is gathering strength behind the surface, and hence will need a heavy bombardment of chemo to retreat or (unlikely) to disappear.

The moods certainly swing. Sometimes all is gentle energy and peace. The clouds lift. Normality returns. But then I can enter an empty time and find myself a bit adrift, lost, confused, wondering how to cope. I can lack interest in anything, reading, seeing people, even praying. But that does not last too long (as yet). A big change is that I have suddenly in these last weeks abandoned my urge to prepare. All my life I have been preparing talks, meetings, events, writings. Now I have only myself to prepare for battle. I feel that this time cancer will win, sooner rather than later. And I can say that calmly and even with a certain strength of spirit. The truth can set free. In all this I am sent angels: people who write to me from Rome or Vietnam or elsewhere. And the message is one of care and love and gratitude: it gives me courage. What is confirmed for me in these conversations is that my overall serenity is not escapist, but real. It is not just an avoidance of darker emotions.

The other day I saw a TV programme, an interview between Gay Byrne and Stephen Fry. In fact my urologist mentioned it to me and I found it. It became famous for Fry's angry diatribe against a monster god, answering Byrne's last question about what he would say to God if he found God waiting for him after death. He would attack him. Did not this god invent an insect that specialised in making children blind? And so on. Some people thought it blasphemous. I don't think he said anything that is not in Dostoevsky, in the mouth of Ivan, rejecting a god who would allow terrible suffering of innocent children. In fact Fry said that he was bi-polar and had tried to kill himself twice. He also seemed bi-polar about religion. He was surprisingly positive about Pope Francis, said he respected those who had religious belief, and came across as a genuine if troubled man. It was strange to watch that interview after receiving my own news of a 'nasty' tumour. Did God send me this cancer? No. Does God want me to face this cancer? Yes. Is God with me promising companionship in the darkness? Yes. Does this change the whole image of death? Certainly yes. And especially in the light of Christ, dying and rising for us. For Fry he was just a prophetic figure who said some strange things. So yes: faith is another story, another horizon, offering a whole other dimension to the experience of this illness. There are cells going mad inside me. It may be too late to stop them. I don't know. What I do know, even dimly at times, is that all this makes sense in a larger picture of things. 'I know in whom I have placed my trust.' That is the difference between me and Stephen Fry. He seemed a good and generous man in spite of all his understandable rage, and that can be his anchor of something like 'salvation'.

He said at one stage: this is all there is, make the most of it. These days I can say that differently. This is all there is for now: make the most of life and love. But in faith this life here is not all there is. Even now there is another presence and power, however shy, and with Christ I trust that death has lost its sting, and is no longer the same shadow on life. On one level I am clearly aware that this cancer may prove fatal. It would be rare to win a third time. On another level I feel a strange freedom and readiness to say good-bye.

Nearly mid-February

Within a week or so I should begin chemo. Both physically and psychologically I veer between 'sailing' and 'sinking'. Sailing means confidence, clarity, trust, relaxed in myself, and here the door into faith and prayer is open and even easy. Sinking means a collapse of attitude, even a sinking feeling in the stomach. It is provoked even by small disappointments or signs of trouble: some blood in the urine, a bit of pain, being too much alone. In that loneliness a magnifying glass takes over and something small becomes large. You get all anxious about getting your clothes washed. A bit of coughing becomes a message of new trouble. I think of this chemo as a bombardment not just of enemy territory but causing plenty of civilian casualties: I expect to feel terrible at times, even on a physical level.

Faith is a space of strength but it is not my doing. It is my receiving and recognising of a word, a gift. Without this dimension I fall into self-concern. This afternoon I went for a walk in the cool sun. I found myself gazing at the huge copper beech, well over a century old. In the summer I have so often admired its beautiful russet abundance of leaves. Now it is totally bare and you can see through it. From where I stood to gaze at it, the tree seemed to overhang both the house where I am going to be living for these coming months and the infirmary where I would possibly move to die. It seemed to bless and embrace all possibilities, and I ask for the grace to do the same.

God has never been so steadily real as in these

last weeks. Not intensely. Sometimes eclipsed by small concerns or fatigue. But the overall and surprising reality is rooted in a quiet trust and friendship and gratitude. The Lord is at work in my whole situation and in my response to it.

L. sent me an email that he is praying for the first time in years! One of my favourite atheists and such a warm and good father. Certainly I have only to listen to pick up so many messages of affection and support, and that makes a great difference. I may be physically alone a lot of the time, but not really alone.

In very ordinary moments, like carrying plates into the kitchen, I am aware of my possible near-mortality. Or more simply that I may not live out this year. It gives another colour to everything, not tragic, or sad, but lonely and sombre in spite of the consolation that is never far away.

Am reading an old book by Henri Nouwen on dying (*Our Greatest Gift*). It's simple but helpful. He links dying with 'becoming as a child' in the gospel, in the sense of losing control and having to depend on others including God. It means an end to accomplishment but not to fruitfulness. Prepare for death as you prepare for a birth. Why not? It involves a surrender to powerlessness, a transition from doing to being. Everyone will go this road of vulnerability sooner or later.

I am, dare I say, enjoying God with me in this strange space. There is huge freedom at times, and of course a shrinking into small fears at times too. Each day has its lights and shadows, its pendulum from yes to no. But the 'no' is always weaker, provoked by some lack of energy or vision. The 'yes' music returns, not as joyful acceptance but as quiet readiness – unalone.

'You used to like going to the theatre.' Yes, I used to. 'Sorry I didn't mean it like that.' Typical of the undercurrents of an ordinary conversation. A lot of my life is now 'used to'. There are so many things I will never do again, even if I were to survive for a year or two. Theatre I could go back to. But teaching, leading, deciding, travelling widely, with a busy diary … all that is over. And I am at peace. I thought of the parable of the house on sand or rock: the flood has come and I trust my house is built on good rock, on faith, on the graces of all these years. I believe so, thank God.

Sometimes I can feel a bit like Job at the beginning of his story. Bad news is coming from all sides. So my body is sending different signals of trouble: urine blood, low energy, throat catch, clots danger, dry cough…. And I know that the main tumour is perhaps not included here! Yes, I can become vulnerable to a cluster of problems. But then the cloud lifts. A generous email reaches me. Receiving a kind word helps. Sharing a few light-hearted comments helps others (and me). So don't be surprised by the ups and downs.

15.2.15

A month since I flew to Ireland! How would I live through this time without faith and hope and love? The full faith picture is beautiful and can embrace the inevitable flashes of darkness.

Beginning chemo

16.2.15

Exactly a month after my operation, I learn that I begin chemo tomorrow. It is a strange relief to get this news, to get this started. There is a background music of harmony that overcomes all the bits of panic and fear.

17.2.15

In hospital for three days. It is good to be here. A strange thought. But I am in great peace. A reading from Isaiah 26 spoke to me: 'you keep him in perfect peace whose mind is stayed on you'. As they pour liquid into me to test the kidney flow, I am overwhelmed by the kindness of everyone from the tea boy to the nurses to the admission lady. The care could not be better. And all this is an attempt to save my life. Without this I would be dead in six months.

Nearly 2 pm: I am sitting here with protective drugs dripping into me, in order to begin the heavy artillery very soon. It is strange to recall a similar hospital room in 2002, and to hope for a less severe reaction! But I am in a different moment of my existence, aware that I need to engage in this battle in order to live, and that it may prove only a temporary ceasefire against the cancer. I say all this with ease and inner freedom.

3.15 pm. Just begun chemo. It will last more than three hours. 8 pm. Finished chemo for today and now on a lot of fluid to clean out the negative aspects. Overall in excellent form. Head a little muzzy. Perhaps tired. But alert, relaxed, talking to everyone. Rooted in the mystery. Surprisingly free about long-term outcomes – at least at present. In tune with the beginning of Psalm 26: 'the Lord is light, salvation, stronghold, whom shall I fear?'. But almost ironically comes the next part: when my 'flesh is assailed and eaten up, the enemies will fall'. My body is eaten up by some nasty malignant cells but they are being attacked now too!

Second day: I am in a place of wonder and relief. So far the chemo has been tolerable but of course it is early days. They tell me the steroids will keep me energetic for a few days afterwards, but then I can expect a dip in energy, an increase in tiredness. I begin to realise how so many of the great realities of faith have taken fire in these weeks: revelation, call, presence, promise, mission. But I also see that these dimensions have roots in deep human experiences even with those who are not religious believers.

Came across remark of Rohr's: vulnerability means allowing events to influence you. That sums up where I am, and perhaps what I am allowing to happen. I am not resisting the new impotence or passivity. My life has prepared me for this and I did not know it. By 'this' I don't immediately mean death, even though that must be closer than if this cancer had not happened. I mean a whole different rhythm of time and of heart and of horizon.

I realise that central relationships have changed: to time, space, body, people … I have oceans of time, that sometimes feels free and sometimes empty; I move in more restricted spaces, house, walks, library, seldom city and no outside entertainment; inevitably I become aware of signals from the body, traces of blood in the urine, touches of nausea, mouth dryness, some mucus, and sometimes waves of non-energy; people are kind but treat me differently, sometimes shy, sometimes curious, sometimes afraid to ask how I am, and yet with many here or even by email there is honest and healthy sharing.

And the relationship to God? That is more easy than I ever imagined: sometimes strong, sometimes in the background, but always gently reachable. Prayer is much more receiving than asking, more relaxing and pondering than striving. Phrases from the psalms come alive, especially expressions of trust in trouble or promises of protection or moments of wonder and gratitude over life as gift. As things may get a bit more difficult, I ask to be saved from self-concern, and to live this period in a spirit of mission and companionship. Yes, a Lent as I said of transformation towards costly joy.

Third day after chemo. I am getting used to the oscillations of energy, in the sense that I can get up in the morning refreshed and at ease, and even before breakfast can feel waves of fatigue or inner emptiness. But these don't last, at least not yet. Today is the last day on steroids and so I am artificially supported. Tomorrow the weather forecast for Ireland talks of gales and heavy rain. I might have my own version in these coming days.

Today for prayer I found myself invited into simple silent presence. Background words of the great readings from Isaiah 58 (the promise of 'I am here' if we try to give bread to the hungry...), but really beyond words, or feelings, or images, or music, resting and sensing another Presence embracing me almost secretly. A sense of gentle Trinity.

Slowness takes over. The day is strangely full of small moments: a bit of prayer, of reading, of eating and sleeping, and some meetings and contacts. Today has had more flashes of dullness or dark than before, more dark on the level of physical weakness than of spiritual attitude.

Some stomach pain, tightness. The first sign of this kind. Late February. My first week of this kind, no events in the diary, just waiting and seeing. I am getting used to this strange rhythm of slow living. It can seem empty or without a goal, but that is not true.

I am aware of the challenge of time and space in these coming weeks. It is easy to drift in 'down' thoughts: this is the beginning of a long road towards the end, and to allow a tone of emptiness to take over.

Contemplative in inaction! Even here the glory of God is our being fully alive – in all this weakness or lack of the usual energies. But am also more aware of the desert ahead. Physical weaknesses tempt me to something like depression (like getting up every 90 minutes in the night to pass water). Being sick long-term is very different from short bouts of illness. The inevitable aloneness can become a difficult loneliness. All this is new for me. I hope to find wisdom along the way, learning to stay alive in a time of famine (Psalm 33).

R., my down-and-out friend of many years, was consoling me on the phone. It's a whole new place for you, he said. Don't let it get you down. You mean so much to me. Coming from him, drug addict, alcoholic, illiterate, sometimes suicidal ... it did me good.

Strange how small things can send me up or down in spirits. Managing to install an anti-virus on the computer was a surprising technological success! Going for a walk in the cold sun did me good. And then the non-arrival of medicines from the pharmacy suddenly left me annoyed and even down in physical form. We are so vulnerable on so many levels. I have to live with these unexpected swings and if possible smile at them, offering them to the Lord.

Today was also marked by angels, in the sense of

people who refreshed my vision. A visit from A. was a real blessing. We know one another for perhaps 40 years and there has always been a flow of trust and imagination between us. I was able to speak very openly about the whole adventure, expressing something of surprising strength and also of fragility. It was important and left me with quiet courage and freedom. That is so necessary. Too much solitary pondering is not good.

Perhaps a little weaker this morning, but wiser not to focus on this. There is a strategy of resistance: simply count your blessings. I can list various ills (the humiliation of frequent urine at night, the big effort to go for a walk, the fear of eating the wrong thing, wondering about how to fill the day ...) but what about the other list: no major side effects, a secure and comfortable place, the many supports of friends and medical people, and the possibility of opening throughout each day to God.

I have to go back to hospital for a procedure next week, perhaps for two days. The gut feeling goes down at once. Passivity can be painful. It prunes the ego of security, or plans. But wisdom means waiting, sitting out any immediate reactions. Perspective comes back. Even a little sleep can change the inner tone and give the body strength again. And visiting the inner space of the spirit is an infallible healer of hope.

So many people want to do something for me, like a meal out, a trip somewhere. I resist, perhaps too abruptly, or just with a sad shake of the head. My style is very introspective. When the body is 'down', like a battery that needs recharging, it is hard to come alive in other ways. I do not want to dump my downs on anyone, but rather communicate something of the deeper plot of peace that I experience too.

These last days the body is the boss and asks for

daily obedience. It sends mixed messages of exhaustion but sometimes of lightness. It is so unpredictable. It can seem like a sulky child, uncooperative for no reason, and then in good humour again.

Today was probably my best day recently. Not too many 'waves of fog' as I have begun to describe it – the graph of flow and flatness of mood, but rooted in the body ... Energy is definitely better than it was, which is a relief. I am less worried about my status as being 'sick'. I am able to write and I am reading more than before. Almost normal rhythm of life. Less physical messages of weakness. Less thoughts of illness or crisis. And yet the chemo is working away inside... I have a different problem when I am in almost normal energy, different from the times when weakness is felt each day. I don't know what to do with all this time and space. My life seems robbed of purpose, at least of the kind of purposefulness it has had all these years of my active work. It is all the more perplexing because I am not sick in any obvious way, just lacking in aliveness and forced into a situation of retirement.

Early March

My hair is showing signs of falling and the beard for days has been much less than before. Not surprising I can't really complain, and one of my pleasures of yesterday was to go into town and buy two hats in a charity shop! ... I have stopped thinking about death and realise that I may well have a whole other chapter of life.

Thanh Ca whom I met briefly in Vietnam sent me an extraordinary text from Philippians 1:12: I want you to realise that what has happened to me is helping the advance of the gospel. Here St Paul goes on to talk about how being in chains has given him a chance to witness to the Lord. I find this extraordinary coming from a young man of 22 without much education.

Back in hospital for a second cycle of chemo. Strangely at peace. Got my hair cut today: it was falling too much. Here they tell me my reports are very positive and that the good news should continue. Once again the nurses are great. They make you feel at home and listened to.

A mini crisis last night with temperature up to 38 or 100.5. Also feeling weak suddenly. But I slept reasonably well and seem back to the middle range normal this morning. I realise how easy the focus shrinks to worries about what the body will do next. And that shrinking of horizon was healed by re-reading Philippians chapter: all about living for Christ but dying being a gain, and which to prefer... Magnificent. I read it in bed with my fever and it was a source of largeness and reality.

Listlessness takes over, with touches of nausea (not really getting sick, but a tightness with occasional burp tendencies ...). This is rougher than before, and the temptation is to get caught in the physical, allowing it to invade moods and become the measure of life. All kinds of spiritual skills are needed to keep perspective. Otherwise a sort of mild depression can dominate the day, and concerns for the body can monopolise attention. Even closing one's eyes for prayer can make me immediately more aware of the various physical zones of unease. I have to acknowledge them but enlarge the size of the tent.

I look at myself in the mirror and each time I get a shock. This bald punk is a new image. But it's also a sure sign of trouble. The chemo this time is already leaving me a bit more fragile physically and emotionally, and yet four steroid tablets seem to have boosted me. It's strange, even sad, to be dependent on chemicals, unfree in a way. Perhaps after eating or sleeping, all is alert and easy, and then unpredictably a bit of nausea or overall lethargy can take over, ruling the mood as from a throne. As St Ignatius says about desolation, it is important to trust that the negative times will not last, that dawn will return, and above all that I am accompanied even inside the dullness of spirit. All is a call to learn love, to learn to allow God's love into the dark cave of anxiety or emptiness.

13.3.15

Getting out of hospital was great but it is hard to describe the facing of each day, especially when this morning I did not want to eat much or do much. ... I am to speak (on Skype) to Bernard running a refugee camp in Jordan in a few minutes. That should put my ailments in the shade ... It did. But inner heaviness continues, relieved again by meals and talking a bit, and no doubt by steroids (which can cause mood swings they warn about). I can feel old, empty, purposeless, alone, and yet that is not the whole story, humanly or spiritually or even with myself.

14.3.15

Better energy today I think. Some of yesterday felt like sleepwalking as a chemo zombie. I felt awful, groggy, distant, weak. And yet it could have been worse. Just a slowness of attention and focus. But after the fog, mental clarity comes back unexpectedly. Last night I decided to watch a DVD of *The Marriage of Figaro* (at least the first act). It was sheer joy. Beauty and life are signs of Resurrection.

Now a certain joy is full in this time of weakness. It is good to have come here to this space and to sense the presence of Christ here. A quiet liberation is taking place. Familiar words ring with depth and promise.

This morning was the almost total eclipse of the sun, which I saw on TV while the outside cloudy world here was cooler and darker. Amazing when you think of it. Sense of immensity. Pointer towards the utter transcendence of God. Yes, I am drawn to that, and it is Jesus who translates that mystery of the Father for us. Faith for now involves getting used to a mixture of intimate clarity and painful fog. Yes, I have to be patient with God! Or rather with my impoverished receiving apparatus.

22.3.15

VISIT TO ROME (To clear out my room, which I was determined to do myself). Well, I am back, and in great consolation. The welcome from the community drew tears to my eyes. You have put into my heart a greater peace, joy and love than I would have ever had on another road of life. I am moved by the welcome, the help, and simply by seeing everyone, even the place itself. And the practical side made giant steps of clearing my room.

I survived a great evening. The special community Mass was deep for me, with the sacrament of the sick and the prayers of the community. My words at the end were somewhat emotional, but that was understood I think.

Now back in Dublin things are a little lonely and bleak. I feel a bit tired in ways that I did not all this week. It will mean an adjustment.

30.3.15

I go back into hospital this evening. Calm about it all. I am aware of some background music of worry. This is going to get tougher.

Here I am again doing chemo at this very moment. Everyone is so kind. Tonight I feel a bit sick and down. It has been a more difficult day in hospital than I had before. Many medicines and a fuzzy sense of everything. Is this the famous nausea? Controlled and suppressed by all the medicines?

John 13 (Holy Thurs): As the chemo pumps into me, I know that in all this battle zone a new 'hour' has come for me, a new perspective on living and dying. In writing I hope to carry His peace to those who live with the shadow of death. It is a shadow that I have seen through in these weeks: it loses its sting when I keep my eyes on the Crucified and Risen Lord.

On a comic note, I notice that I still have an urge to comb my non-existent hair, and I even carry a comb in my pocket as I have done for years. I have stopped being surprised seeing my bald self in the mirror but often before going downstairs I have the urge to tidy the hair! Habits die hard.

Good Friday evening

A little groggy, fuzzy, sleepy but okay. Pondering the Passion I am struck by the profound loneliness of the Lord, especially in the Agony, but perhaps all his life in ways. On balance I think I may survive another year or two, and if so I ask to know my calling: what to do in this gift of extra time?

A CANCER DIARY

A pleasant evening in another community where people were very warm and understanding. But I was largely up and down, even during the meal. Sometimes clear and alert, sometimes physically rotten and struggling to focus. I suppose it is the first day after steroids and the impact of side effects is at its strongest. It could be worse I know. Possibly the therapy is accumulating more than other weeks, leaving me low and listless. Just a bit washed out, even though the downs are not steady. But at the same time serene, unworried, carrying each day's burden quietly with the Lord.

I am looking for a good word for my struggle with fatigue: unalert, sleepy, empty head, sagging spirit ... I need to get used to it, I imagine, whether it is cancer-fatigue or chemo-impact, it may easily increase in coming weeks. As Rowan Willliams has written, we cannot experience healing without deepening our hurt. There is a dark road of transformation surrounding me in these months, so that it is wrong to settle into a more comfortable cohabitation with sickness or danger. I need to open myself to the lonely shadows of fragility and even fear. The unknown roads of pain and non-control need to be surrendered to the Lord. This is a more demanding grace of trust in tune with the darker music of now. Perhaps silent presence is the best language of honesty in such moments.

To enter the strangeness needs a different wavelength of silence, vulnerability and prayerful hunger. Will I see another Easter? I don't know. Possibly, but the whole future is fragile. The ordinary life of these days needs the courage to recognise a background music of pain and perplexity, the shock waves even when they seem to have become familiar. I have a possibly fatal illness. Full stop. And I want to live this deeply and worthily.

15.4.15

Three months exactly since I arrived in Ireland and went to emergency in the hospital. So much changed so suddenly. And I have seemed to cope almost with ease. There were no depths of despair or shock. From the beginning I embraced reality with a kind of calm trust, and as that reality revealed itself as cancer, even to a dangerous degree, it never really disturbed my roots of faith and peace. Of course there were moments of feeling down, depressed, lonely, lost, fragile and so on. But the overall tone of heart was peaceful, even prayerful. When I try to listen, I find myself accompanied by God. In all likelihood I will die sooner rather than later. Something in me fears a feeble old age, but I have to leave all that in God's hands.

21.4.15

In hospital. As I arrived last night I found myself spontaneously praying, not for any intention, but just to recall and enjoy the companionship of the Lord in all this. And people have been very kind and helpful here all night. I am due to have a scan this morning, which could be crucial for future possibilities. I remain surprisingly calm with a kind of quiet obedience to reality as the call of God. And with a fairly constant background music of Presence or trust. What does it ask of me except gratitude and attention?

Later: I did my scan and am at this very moment

having chemo. I remain strangely free about whatever news emerges and about whatever future beckons.

GOOD NEWS. Dr McD came in to say that the scan showed improvement all round. The shadows are lessening, etc. But I am still in level 4 and that I should be cautious about planning any journeys because the side effects usually accumulate. Even today after a good walk to the sea in the sun, and a sense of the Lord in the chapel, I went 'down' with some initial nausea for a short time. But the prayer in the chapel was simple: I thank you for the wonder of my being.

I wrote a decent poem today 'As chemo pumps away'. Perhaps this mild burst of creativity is born from my new freedom for attentiveness and my new absence of time pressures.

It looks as if I am not going to die this year. But I may never go back to the old rhythm of productivity and preparation, or indeed to some of my typical themes and concerns. I feel drawn to write about the spiritual side of faith and with a certain creativity of language. Indeed I notice that these jottings have changed from a diary of cancer to a more spiritual focus.

26.4.15

Again rather washed out in terms of energy. It was much the same three weeks ago. B. is visiting here (as a break from his work with refugees in Jordan) but I find it hard even to listen at length. Yes I am both low and lonely, perhaps mildly depressed not just physically. The chemo is accumulating I imagine, winning its destructive battle but at a price. Prayer can only be a kind of honest survival in dim trust.

27.4.15

This journey is going to get tougher it seems. I feel old, weak, fragile, on the decline. Even with touches of depression. Perhaps a little less so this morning, but nevertheless I am gradually entering a more shrunken space of life. There are less stimuli from people, emails, phone calls ... I don't want to go out much. It is important not to worry others with my heaviness. I can be honest but with lightness of tone.

Later: The energies quietly rise. It is amazing how different I am from this time yesterday, not just physically but in terms of aliveness, gratitude, hope.

28.4.15

The dull weather continues in every sense. Perhaps I am beginning to recognise the sea-change in my life. What seemed so ordinary and everyday for years is gone for ever: the pressures of reading and writing and speaking. The teacher or speaker may never be active again. Instead I am in Ireland, more deprived of prospects than ever. Not depressed but increasingly struck by the strange absence of goals or external calls. Today I was physically down at various times and sometimes grumpy or fed up, a bit resentful or ungenerous in my reactions.

Later: I recognise a battle between two forms of smallness. I can be petty, resentful, mean, ungenerous, self-anxious and self-concerned. The illness with its interaction of physical and psychological fragility tempts me into this worried mood. But if I embrace the limits of now, the difficulties are carried in companionship with Christ. The humiliating moments of fatigue or numb void are not removed but become a cross shared with Him. All this threshold of impotence is a frontier where reality calls me to 'lose' my hold on life, my familiar control of everything, and open my situation to the hidden action of God.

No miracles change the horizon. The clouds continue. The consolation is dark. It does not deny or suppress the pain. But it surrenders to Another in trust. It is fairly new for me to experience such daily physical weakness or numbness, as opposed to various kinds of vulnerability.

There is a zone of myself that is far from converted by grace: it welcomes what suits my needs and can be distant and withdrawn in a non-welcoming way to anything or anyone that does not burn incense before my little idol of ego. These times of weakness challenge my lack of generous welcome in so many situations. I have always been goal-driven, with clear purpose in each day, but now I don't have a purpose, not even my own survival. Fear tempts me again and again into falsities of tone or mood or self-protection. It is 'towards evening' and it is time to 'remain' through the time to come. Many old doors are closed, many old chapters will never be revisited. But something precious is possible and coming into focus. I need to ask and seek and light will be given.

4.5.15

Struck by the sentence in the gospel: 'I have food you know not of'. It is true. Today I looked at a photo of the Bellarmino College on an outing. I looked at so many familiar faces smiling, and I sensed the mystery of so many of them. I miss them and yet that feeling is more of gratitude than sadness. It has been a blessing to serve there, to give what I could, even within my limitations. Now suddenly that space is no more. The memories are joyful. The letting go is a bit painful but it is my call, my reality.

5.5.15

I was reading a short story in bed about scans for cancer and level 4. It was a bit disturbing. It reminds me that my cancer remains dangerous in spite of the shrinking of the tumours. Today the end of Psalm 32 was very real: 'The Lord looks on those who hope in his love ... to keep them alive in famine ... Without faith how could I live this? Not that faith is a shield but it is a wider story of love and hope.

11.5.15

Off to hospital again in a few hours. Some days ago I felt a lot of resistance and even physical distaste for all this treatment. But now I am more at ease and at peace even though this is a lonely road.

The day got more difficult. For the first time I was off my food. This chemo hit faster and more heavily. Hard to pray. Easier to watch soccer! But I am never far from quiet trust.

15.5.15

The stuff is pouring into me. Definitely a tougher time on this visit. I expect troubled days ahead. Already I sense a collapse of normal energy. A struggle to reach alertness.

The body feels like a battlefield.

Aware of how different my situation. It really does matter how long I have to live. There is freedom there, although I need to avoid an uncaring indifference. I have something to do with the precious time I am given.

Today is one of the most 'down' days I have had. Predictable perhaps. It leaves me struggling with something akin to depression but able to relax into quiet attending and even some good moments of honest expression. I do not want to burden anyone with my feelings of fragility. At Mass in the infirmary I felt myself totally a member of that group of frail old men, lost and almost dozing in a limbo, but at the end clarity of head returned. Faith can be so blank and without light. Just a tired hanging in there. God makes no tangible difference to the body's situation. In my head I debate between better to live or better to die. All this time is putting a belt around me and drawing me into unknown spaces of weakness and insecurity, and into a breakthrough into humble trust. This situation invites me to surrender and simplicity, not self-effort.

28.5.15

I am now emerging into a different space of hope. Energy is nearly normal. 'Who would have thought my shrivelled heart could have recovered greenness?' (Herbert's poem 'The Flower'.) I am envisaging life rather than death.

The news today is of the death of Vice-President Biden's son at 46 of brain cancer. They say he responded well to treatment but then it came back. I saw similar figures for lung cancer on TV recently. Realistically, I should see myself as granted a period of protection or successful resistance to the cancer, but long term? I will probably see Christmas

2015 but 2016? These thoughts give me a gentle urgency to make best use of the time, spiritually and creatively. Without forcing but without wasting.

1.6.15

Back in hospital for my sixth session of three days. The hospital chapel is not far from the cancer corridor. I found myself there alone and not alone. Here I am strengthened beyond any human logic. Here I find a strange space of friendship and trust. Many would say it is all a fairy-tale illusion. Others have lost contact with spaces of faith. I simply know that I receive light and consolation. I do not come for that. I come for Him, to be with Him, to open to His call. And now I have the space and spirit to do so – a real luxury that I never had before like this.

Hearing some cancer stories on the radio, I am convinced that this period of chemo will give me months of something like remission, but the cancer seems likely to come back with more force. And if so, I would not want to offer total resistance to the coming of death. I am clear and happy with this, hoping perhaps to have another year from now.

During a walk outside, severe chest pain, which happened before during chemo-time. Back to here, and could only listen to some radio poetry. But then a chat with the night nurse lifted me again. I suppose it is a mixed battlefield, relational, psychological, physical, spiritual. But it is great to come to the end of all this chemo.

I sometimes think that the chemo effects are a preparation for the process of dying: it will surely involve these unexpected falls into impotence. I was filled with a lonely sense of death. In spite of friends and even of faith I'm going to die feeling alone. The night psalm answered this: 'When he calls I shall answer, "I am with you"', I will save him in distress'. Not alone and yet feeling alone.

It continually surprises me how these post-chemo reactions can change suddenly from heaviness to ease, and back again. These days I am returning to good energy and spiritually I find myself enjoying deep silence when I prepare reverently. At times I even imagine that my health could be on the mend, and that death might not be that close.

1.7.15

The scan shows that the original tumour in the bladder has almost disappeared but the secondary shadows in the liver continue to exist. They are smaller than before, but probably will return with more strength sooner or later. The question is when. So the proposal is to have a two-month gap, with no treatment, and to do another scan at the beginning of September. I am happy with all this, but fully aware that the battle is not over, and that there may be tougher times later on. I see that I am living a special moment of freedom, where gratitude can and should be dominant. I look back with thanksgiving on how I have been able to live and give. Perhaps this is another strand in the chemo journey: the lull after the desert times. I seem simply more at ease with reality and in particular with spiritual knowledge of God's presence each day. So seize the day, or the week, or the month, whatever is granted.

28.7.15

A fright today. After being in town for a while, had a sharp pain in left back during lunch. It got worse and moved to the front when I lay down. But thank God it has gone after a rest. What is interesting is the level of my lonely fear: here we go again. It brings home the fragility of the body and of the spirit, and indeed of the level of faith.

August

During this seeming remission I write less of this diary. Instead I work in the other parts of the book. Life flows happily, almost as if there were no danger ahead. It is harder to believe that I could be seriously ill or going towards death. Perhaps I am not. The body is giving no signals of trouble at present.

Early September

Had a scan today. I found myself praying as I waited in the little cubicle, blessed with great peace about where all this is leading. I am in God's hands at this stage in everything … Was able to have four days in Amsterdam, with two Jesuit contemporaries and friends. Went really well and in good energy. But on return the news is not great. I more or less expected it. The remission was disappointingly short, said Dr McD. The shadows on the liver have doubled. He suggested more chemo, but less heavy than before, perhaps one day at a time, beginning in about two weeks. I told him I was not unduly worried. He asked if I had any projects to finish (perhaps a revealing question). I told him about a book called 'Into Extra Time'. We laughed. He also promised to tell me if he thinks that continuing chemo is not worth it. In other words (my interpretation) it will be terminal, with some postponements. After just ten minutes with him, I went to the hospital chapel and thanked the Lord for the wonder of my being, asking only to be blessed with a sense of his companionship in all this. I drove back calmly in heavy traffic. Perhaps it hasn't really struck yet. I wonder about how much to tell people. Enough to say to people that the liver secondaries need more chemo, but a lower dose this time.

Perhaps I had hoped that the remission would be stable for longer. But thank God for the graces of these weeks and months. I am ready for decline or at least I hope so. And I am eager to enjoy what is left with the Lord. I told the small community at the evening meal, lightly and towards the end. I think they got the message. When Liam said to me later 'You are amazing', I replied 'I am amazing myself, or rather the Spirit is amazing me'. For the first time I feel certain that I will die within a year or less. My prayer is, 'Stay with me, it is towards evening and the day is almost spent'.

I had a great conversation with M., one of my oldest and most sensitive friends. He realised at once that yesterday's news is serious. He asked, as most people don't dare, about my feelings. I was able to say that yes I am at peace but it is also strange and lonely at times. I mentioned people I worry about, who will suffer from my death, including him. Most people are sympathetic but stay on the externals of medical developments. To have time for the heart to be expressed and recognised is rare but beautiful. This year I have known this ease more with women than men, but there are men too thank God.

Late September

Today for the first time a nurse mentioned that this chemo

could be more palliative than curative. It struck home and left me for a while with a sinking feeling in the stomach. There are some convergent signs that I am in decline: loss of weight, confusion of words more than before, cough, bits of stomach or back pain, more easily tired. Have the cells gone on the rampage in other organs?

Got out to a play by a cousin of mine and enjoyed it. But the sense of an ending is more frequent, more daily, more ordinary. It is hard when I cannot seem to enter the nourishing space of prayer. But then the clouds open and light comes in spite of unworthiness.

I find tears in my eyes seeing Pope Francis among the prisoners of Philadelphia. I would like to offer my bearing of my cross for him. I feel 'rotten' at times, almost as when after chemo but I haven't begun this cycle! Inwardly here is a transition from activity to passivity, but always with a promise of the Lord's presence, even in a dim twilight of body and spirit.

This latest phase leaves me a bit down, worried in a way. It could mean a faster departure from this world than I imagined. Facing this head-on is good, and it leads to a different trust in the Lord, expressed more in ordinary life than in separate times of prayer. How easily the body can undermine consolation, not always but usually. There is a less clear sense of the Spirit in the midst of weaknesses. As I have the impression of different parts of the body joining in a mini-rebellion, I accept a more muddled prayer in this situation of more feebleness.

I prayed today with the last passage of Romans 8. The core is so strong: nothing like tribulation or danger or sword can separate us from the love of Christ, and I can change Paul's list: illness, decline into tiredness of life, possible trouble in lung or brain as well as the liver, and ultimately the increasing likelihood of death sooner.

And in all this, mentioning death itself, says St Paul, we are victorious through Him who loved us. That is an extraordinary promise. Indeed I notice a shift in focus from presence to promise.

Early October

Once again E. had the woman's touch. She let me admit that I am at a low ebb and feel frightened in a new way. Never except during chemo times have I felt so washed out. It is a great change from the situation from even two weeks ago. That combination of alarm bells mount up. I wonder if I will ever return to normality, the ease I enjoyed during the last few months. But it was great to be heard and understood.

They ordered a brain scan because of my increase of mistakes in words. A special moment was when I dragged myself to the chapel in the hospital before the scan: there was total lift of spirit, with peace, gratitude, courage to face whatever with Christ. It can stay as background music when my whole system seems dog tired.

3.10.15

Most of the day in some kind of pain, mainly back and stomach, and bowels a bit frequent. And above all, low in energy. But I found a language of prayer to suit this sickish moment.

4.10.15

Tomorrow chemo. I don't think I am in great form for this. My generally low form leaves me nervous. These last two weeks bring a new situation to cope with, psychologically and spiritually. I sleep well but in the morning the various areas of distress come alive. Eating is forced. I read that God is love, full of compassion to those who call from the heart. All this I trust but there is filter, no fire. When minor pains dominate, it is hard not to have some self-concern. Pain blocks steady prayer.

5.10.15

I started day chemo. It is to be one day a week and then a week free. I found it very different to the in-stay hospital – in a long room of about thirty cancer patients, mainly women. Many of them had companions with them. I was alone. In spite of my list of symptoms I was told that the chemo could go ahead. It started with protections.

Personally it was a tough day, lonely, tired, yet able to find an important anchor for prayer. I have tried to be a companion of Jesus all my life. Now I offer my slow journey of letting go, asking that that my bits of darkness be united with Christ's agony. I can only offer my numb road to His cross where pain is beyond all imagination. From Him I learn how to face this chapter, one I am convinced is in decline.

Am I depressed? Possibly. The love behind Jesus on the Cross was not full of joy or light. It was a kenosis or pouring out, a self-emptying.

6.10.15

Overnight an important addition to my insight of yesterday. It is so simple, I'm surprised I didn't see it. When I am cast down by low energy or difficulties to face in silence, instead of resenting some spiritual intensity that is not possible, I embrace this weakness as a strange gift. I recognise now that it was a temptation to remain cast down instead of seeing my tiny and slower passion sharing in his great Passion. I was inclined to turn in on myself in spiritual impotence, when a quieter attention seemed out of reach.

8.10.15

The physical ups and downs are predictable. My death, all death, is evil but it is also life. Externally my dying is tough and alone each day, but in my dying I am called to carry my cross with Christ's, to learn new love there, to be placed with Christ carrying his Cross. Easier prayed in short moments than head steadily in the ordinary winds.

LATER: P., an imaginative friend since he was a student of mine many years ago, came to see me for the first time for some months. His first words were 'You're looking more worn and you've gone hoarse'. 'Yes, thanks for being direct', I said, 'and I am mixing up my words too'. As the conversation went on, I stumbled more and more on words. With P., who is not a conventional believer, it was a freedom to speak openly of my decline of these last weeks, and to admit that I might sink faster than

I expected. This honesty is more helpful than skirting around issues for fear of upsetting one another. But it needs the right space or right friend. Certainly I feel mourning at the speech difficulty, since I have always relished words. Goodbye to one of my gifts. Later this evening they commented that my voice at Mass was uncertain during one of the readings.

Brain tumour: terminal

8.10.15

A kind phone call from my oncologist came when I was having a late breakfast. There are 'spots' on the brain. He mentioned consulting a radiation specialist and two kinds of radiation, one more focussed and other more generalised and heavy. I immediately said let's consult and wait and see. I asked one obvious question: Is it now terminal? Yes. So how much time, something between three and six months? Very likely he said. I knew already but this clarity brought great peace.

I interrupted breakfast and went to the chapel. Today happens to be the anniversary of my entry to the Jesuits. I repeated my promises with quiet joy, asking the Lord to stay close at this time. As I write this the radio is playing lively Vivaldi and outside the sun is brilliant on the changing autumn leaves of gold and red. I am only worried about the impact of the news on others. However two hours later I dipped into nervousness and even trembling. I think it is more physical than psychological. Today's news has its effect, but not destroying the inner serenity.

Later: I told three people, including with special freedom with M. But the day overall was a yo-yo. An inner numbness may have been caused by the withdrawal from steroids, no doubt the lonely impact of the truth, and some anxiety of losing my speech.

9.10.15

Half-asleep often today. Diarrhoea. Speech slowed or

confused. Difficult to focus in prayer. A real sinking in energy. Afraid of meeting people. No spiritual ease but just holding up my situation as offering.

10.10.15

Still struggling with dullness. Time of ease, even of prayerfulness. I mix Psalms 'out of the depths' and 'The Lord is my Shepherd'. Some real surrender and trust, thank God. But physically down, stomach tight, eating little, falling asleep. Difficult to talk to visitors. I talked openly to Dr D. that I might consider suspending treatments. Why ask for radiation if it only causes more side effects and does not improve my speech power? I'm alone but in spite of heaviness, strangely at peace in the troubles. Not the old peace but better focus and sense of God. I was touched by P. in China who seemed to weep at the mention of my dangers of death.

11.10.15

A down day mostly. Fatigue, nausea, sickish, lost in vague pain ... I am inclined to discontinue chemo and not to begin radiation. I ask the Lord to give me light and courage. In some moments of clarity and consolation today I seemed confirmed in this decision. It is tough all round, even though I do my best to keep out a good side.

12.10.15

Slowly but surely I move towards a decision: to stop chemo and opt for palliative care. I am at peace with the Lord, having talked with my Provincial (religious superior) and with the health people. I felt that I did not need a course of radiation, even if it means I become more confused in language. Even already writing these days I have more difficulty, where I never had any problems with words. I said to E. on the phone that I miss the focus of clarity for praying and he replied many will be praying for me. You can be carried by others here and hereafter. Yes, it is a time for handing over, trusting, surrendering, and today I sense that the Lord will carry me even if I cannot feel anything.

Palliative care

14.10.15

Perhaps this is the biggest decision of all these ten months. I told the team that I did not want to return to chemo, because of the severe effects last week and because the cancer zones are already terminal and I am not likely to improve significantly. Dr D. after some questions agreed. It was a sensitive conversation and he will be a guide in the background even though I now pass to the palliative team. They too visited me and were equally kind and helpful. They will put me under a dietician for the moment, and in a few weeks we will see what palliative care is needed. All in all I was blessed with such meetings. And in myself I felt myself confirmed in this crucial choice. I seemed able to pray gently most of the day, with a sense of being confirmed by the Good Spirit and asking to be accompanied in this last phase and the approach of death. Of course there will be down and lost moments. The nurse came to check my blood pressure after the oncologist left. I asked how it was and she said a little high, but what would you expect after such a life-changing conversation! She also remarked that people who are happy in themselves often make this kind of decision with more serenity.

15.10.15

Ten months exactly since my night in emergency. Today had its dips into low energies but they emerged with exercise, food, medicine. Tonight a great gift. I was dreading telling my Italian friend P., who was my closest companion for 24 years in Rome. I phoned and was able to tell him gently the whole story, and when I said to him that I had been worried about telling him, he said that I had helped him find strength (for instance at the difficult time of the birth of his daughter, at only 23 weeks of pregnancy; she was named Michela after me). It was great to hear him able to take my situation on board, even though I know he suffers from this loss. I went to the chapel to thank the Lord for such a friend with his own not very church-going but prayerful faith.

I discover that when I am alert, I can pray with quiet joy and gratitude, and when I enter some of the inner fogs I remember St Paul saying when you cannot pray, the Spirit will pray within you.

16.10.15

Possibly weakness will be permanent and alertness comes for short periods. Prayerfully, when I can, I offer my present emptiness and numb spirit. People are sad but supportive. I feel I have aged ten years in less than one year. I expect new complications ahead, sooner or later. I have no idea of how long this declining phase will last. I might not reach Christmas, but remain in the hands of the Lord.

17.10.15

The body found more energy and clarity. Perhaps the new tablets are kicking in. What was important was the ability to enjoy reflection and prayer, even with something like tears of joy and gratitude. It was a gift of strength, hard to describe. Probably it can't last but 'of his fullness we have all received'. It was as if the Lord knocks at the door to enter and I was so blessed to open. Intimacy and freedom were silently embracing.

19.10.15

A good Sunday, with now usual highs and lows. I appreciated a talk with J. who had been away these weeks from the community. He was sensitive and listening, and I could even admit that there are deep emotions and tears, fragile tears. Then later P. gave me a drive to the sea and while he had a brisk walk, I revisited the disused swimming pool where I learned to swim and looked into the hotel (now offices) where I went many summers for childhood holidays. A visit into memories, happy ones. What touched me is that I can mix terminal illness and much thanksgiving for the past, the present and indeed this strange journey towards death. A phase where Christ walks with me and at the end awaits me. It is difficulty to express it. At times it is so strong, even though at times my tiredness eclipses it. I also spoke on Skype or had messages from various people. They tell me that I have lived a certain freedom all these years. It leaves me touched in a way that is both joyful and vulnerable.

19.10.15

Feast of St Isaac Jogues and those Jesuit martyrs who were so terribly tortured. My body runs into exhaustion but it is nothing. I realise that God loves me and suffers, in a sense, from not being able to reach me. My states of dullness do not last, and in flashes that embrace touches me, where love holds my weakness. Does this make sense to anyone else? Perhaps not.

A CANCER DIARY

The wavelengths seem to swing more strongly. There are tunnels of lonely exhaustion when I seem unwilling to cross the room but they don't last more than an hour or so. Remembering a word of prayer, both body and mood rise, like a healing surprise of being unalone. Sometimes it ripens into joy and thanksgiving, recalling so many blessings and gifts. I rest in peace, love, thanksgiving. Even the body seems to find strength, or to be less crushed by its forms of heaviness. Hard to put into words, but it happens.

22.10.15

The situation is not easing. I have normally slept long nights (with visits to the toilet of course) but now it is a bit more disturbed, and woken by a very dry mouth. Hard to stimulate myself to eat. Such petty complaints. Not able for many visitors and yet it is good when they come. I am grateful and moved for their care. Into all this the Lord promises a certain 'sweetness' when I can gather an openness of heart. I go round in circles in these recent jottings. Has the time come to take a pause and wait for another phase of consolation?

23.10.15

An unexpected day. Because of some blood in the urine Dr D. advised coming into hospital for a few days. For me a difficult day of waiting, weakness, tests, disappointment and perhaps for the first time I use the word depression. But blessed by a surprising grace towards evening, after getting impatient at being left so alone for hours awaiting a room. The nurse in charge of me must have passed 20 times dealing with others, and never saying anything to me. I tried to ask the possibility of quietly accepting, but it was not easy. Then at one point she said a bed would be ready. I asked would there even be a meal at this late hour. Something cold surely. On her return I apologised about my tone of complaint. Not at all, she said. Suddenly my long struggle of moods eased. I was able to wait passively with a sense of the Lord. A light of consolation took over, even with deep feeling. The Paul insight that when I am weak then I am strong. It was carried gently by this presence of the Spirit for the rest of the day. I am still low in strength but again the spirit is lifted.

25.10.15

Two months to Christmas. Will I still be here? I wonder. A bit frustrated that I am still in hospital for a third night. I had a low and drifting day without focus, just taking medicines I have at home. I felt lonely, impotent, numb most of the time, and with little desire for food. I hope tomorrow to raise the question of going home. But the day had its graces. When they brought me communion, I found myself praying from the heart: 'you come to bring me home'. That was full of trust and thanks. Later when S. came on as night nurse, I outlined my downs to her and she was so warm and receptive of my feelings and difficulties. Again another sacrament that just heals the struggling self.

28.10.15

I managed to get home. A real relief, even though I am

weaker than before and speak more slowly at times. Poor appetite. Not able for long visits. In general I sink in energies. I ask people to pray that I have enough physical alertness to enjoy the Lord consciously at times. Many months ago I began these jottings about 'waves of fog', when I was mainly describing the impact on my mood of chemo. Now it is more a physical confusion of exhaustion caused by the medicines and the aches and dips of the cancer itself. I hope I have conveyed an unstable struggle – spiritual, bodily and psychological. It is an ancient experience. The psalms are so full of honest expressions of struggle like this. 'An enemy crushes my life to the ground ... dwelling in darkness ... my heart is numb within me ... Like a parched land my soul thirsts for you ... Let your good spirit guide me ... In the way of my distress I sought the Lord ...' (Psalms 142 and 76).

I don't know if I will have strength to continue these jottings fruitfully much further or with lucidity. Perhaps a friend will add a few words. May the reader receive some light and pray for me. Thank you.

'Perhaps a friend will add ...'

Friday 30 October. His computer got stuck as Michael Paul finished the Diary, and he wasn't able to edit it any more. He gave me a memory stick to edit on another machine, and then said, 'It is over, the book is done! I am ready to go!' The next week would be memorable for me and for many, as were the long years of friendship, advice, good fun, prayer.

The weekend of 31 October – 1 November was a tough one. He had a lot of pain, and also confusion, and was well looked after in his Jesuit community. He returned to hospital on the Monday and for a number of hours the confusion continued until, I think, the painkillers found the balance and he was more at peace.

2 – 6 November. A few people visited Michael Paul briefly and we spoke a little. When I dropped into the hospital, his speech was now troubling him, but we thanked each other for our long friendship. He asked for a blessing, and then he blessed me and we embraced. That was among his last conversations. Later conversations were somewhat confused and sometimes unclear, with great difficulty in speaking. Jesuits and other close friends visited, as well as cousins, and at this point he wished only for those he was closest to. Palliative care was doing for him what needed to be done.

6 November. Some visited him briefly during the day. He was comfortable, though breathing heavily. I visited at about 7 pm. He was in a coma, so I have no idea if he could hear me. I prayed a bit with him, and said, 'Let go now – call on the graces of the last months. It's time, as you said'. Someone else came in to visit him then, and later in the evening some of his community, and gradually he became calmer. At about 10 pm, the hospital phoned Milltown, and we got there in time to anoint him, and pray with him as he quietly made the journey, just after we were singing a Taizé chant. His cousins from Meath who had been there earlier were then called, and arrived shortly after he died.

Michael Paul requested that his funeral Mass be in Milltown Park, and that he would not, at any time, have an open coffin. He made no other requests. His funeral service was held on Monday 9 November and

A CANCER DIARY

Tuesday 10 November. Later a huge crowd celebrated his memorial Mass in the packed Gesù Church in Rome.

Note. As I reread this book, I gradually realised it is a book about life, as much as about death. It is about letting go, about finding God, about the values and joys of friendship, and about faith. Michael Paul resonated in the last weeks with the words of one of his 'heroes', Teilhard de Chardin SJ: 'we are spiritual beings on a human journey'. May he enjoy the love of the God and Jesus Christ he deeply loved.

Donal Neary
January 2016

4
POETRY

Here are a few attempts at verse, never my talent, perhaps damaged by too much exposure to literary criticism. But they came during the illness and may capture something.

AS CHEMO PUMPS AWAY

Outside, blossom-exploding trees
Sway in sunlight as guarantors of spring.
Inside, my hospital bed spurts
the tubes needed for battle
against invisible beasties.
Purple plastic protects Hilary
as she hooks me up for hours of chemo.
They tell me all is working well:
so I sing a shy *Te Deum*
(in half-remembered Latin).
But my assaulted body looks
to the dancing trees
to kindle embers of hope,
until with eyes closed
another presence lets me
touch a promise stronger
and stranger than tubes or trees
or the ancient beauty of *Te Deums*.

EARTHQUAKES

It sounds like the puff puff trains of my childhood,
going click clik along its rails.
With the window open
you could get smut in your eyes.
Now chemicals pour click clik gently
yet menacingly into my veins,
a savage sort of salvation.
With a two-hour chemo flow underway
I was watching images of the Nepal earthquake
when a lady chaplain came with communion.

INTO EXTRA TIME

I received and stayed still,
knowing that my little seismic upheavals
invite to solitudes of surrender.
But Nepal comes back to haunt: its people
locked beneath their collapsed everything,
with no red buttons to summon nursing help.
'Here's your scrambled eggs, love,
High protein will do you good'.
Syria, Iraq, Libya, Lampedusa...
Amid scenes of man-made horror,
cushioned mortality leaves me
uneasy with such spoiling.
But click clik, click clik continues
With its mix of blessing and battering.

DEPARTURE DATE
(with thanks to W. S. Merwin)

Without knowing it,
each year I have lived
the departure date,
as will be on my memorial card.
These coming months that day will arrive
with struggle or serenity.
I only know a goodbye must come
and as they close my eyes
and arrange rites of farewell
where will I be?
'I know in whom I place my trust':
More I cannot say,
as I am pruned for
an unimaginable space
where departure can become arrival.

WEATHER FORECAST

Before getting out of bed, this feels like
Another shaky start for an uncertain day.
Unlike the sun outside, the head is cloudy dull.
Perhaps a breakfast egg will do the protein trick,
Raising the chemistry fog, lightening the mood.
But swings happen without warning
From numb to normal and back again,
Leaving me guilty that I can't manage
A convincing smile to disguise unstable weather.

QUARTET

Dr Google the world renowned consultant
Knows everything about cancer
And spouts out blunt statistics
Data you cannot argue with.
I prefer the oncologist's discretion,
But between the lines
The message is the same:
This time we won't win.
How to respond?
Shakespeare puts it best:
Love that well
Which you must leave e'er long,
But Simeon suggests more –
Go in peace
Your hopes fulfilled.
Amen.

BACH ON SKYPE

Who would have imagined
Our easy affection across an ocean?

INTO EXTRA TIME

I recall such an angular Aleardo,
How he sat and spoke edgily
In that little 'parlour' in Rome,
Until another music was recognised
And a miracle crossed
Into thresholds of trust
enriched with years.
In my new fragility
You offer care beyond words,
Able to intuit horizons
You do not share.

Play on dear friend:
I foresee you one day
Fingering a Bach lullaby
For children I will never see.

MONIQUE IN CAEN

The heart carries more than memories:
When I think of you, of us, or see a photo,
All is alive like yesterday.
I wonder what happened to you,
what you did with that tenderness,
With the shy strength of your gaze.
Did the years harden or soften your beauty?
Did you forget me, hurt by my silence
Let down by my different path? Or can you visit,
as I do, wonder echoes
Of hands held and eyes knit,
Symbols of a love bigger than
we were able for at twenty one,
but changing me at least forever.